Dave Coffaro's *Leading* [...] how to pivot and remain rel[...] environment. A must read for leaders, business owners, and consultants looking for a simple, yet effective paradigm for fostering greater resilience, relevance, and revenues.

Kathleen Burns Kingsbury, Wealth Psychology Expert & Author, *Breaking Money Silence®: How to Shatter Money Taboos, Talk More Openly About Finances, and Live a Richer Life*

David Coffaro has written a brilliant book, *Leading from Zero*, which lays out a compelling argument for starting every day with a mindset of zero—which means that to be a great leader at home, work and life requires one to "earn their stripes" every day. He makes a powerful argument that the best of the best leaders never take anything for granted, and they commit to positively touching the hearts, minds, and souls of those around them not once a week, not twice a week, but every single day. The reader will see very quickly why David is one of the most sought-after consultants and coaches in the U.S., as he clearly distills for the reader—as he does in his practice, the seven foundational pillars for earning relevance as a leader. I highly recommend David's book for anyone who wants to become a better leader at work and home!

John Mattone, Founder & Co-Chairman, John Mattone-Global, Inc.

In a world of constant disruptions - think COVID-19 - leaders need to constantly focus on making their organizations relevant to customers, employees, and other stakeholders. In *Leading from Zero*, Dave Coffaro offers a blueprint for how to adapt to an ever-changing environment, stay relevant, and be successful.

Ronald Riggio, PhD, Professor, Kravis Leadership Institute - Claremont McKenna

David Coffaro's Leading from Zero is a powerful mindset that can help individuals and companies not only become competitive but more importantly, remain competitive. With a commitment to working every day in every way to make every interaction powerful and never a given – this approach enables a company to maximize every opportunity. The verve and momentum enabled by the big ideas in the book makes Coffaro's work a difference maker.

Kimberly Janson, PhD., President & CEO Janson Associates

As business leaders, we understand that the environments in which our businesses operate change continually. How do we develop, refine and maintain strategies to keep our organizations relevant without sacrificing our company's vision and values? In Leading from Zero, David Coffaro uses the concept of "zero-based budgeting" as a foundation for exploring how your company can earn its relevance every day. David's use of examples, both public and personal, make this an interesting and easy read, and his specific recommendations will allow you to immediately begin applying your learnings to your business.

Larry Tucker, Board Chair Emeritus, SCORE, a national nonprofit dedicated to starting and growing small businesses.

Dave Coffaro provides a terrific roadmap for strategic thought leadership. He adapts the concept of zero-based budgeting to strategic leadership and provides seven essential elements of earning relevance that are practical and logical. This is a must-read for leaders.

Simone Lagomarsino, President & CEO, Luther Burbank Savings

Dave Coffaro's *Leading from Zero* offers a critical framework to guide social sector leaders grappling with changing community needs, shifting demographics, myriad stakeholders and an increasingly competitive funding environment. While nonprofits are, by their very definition, cause driven, urgency of mission does not always translate into relevance in the market of community services, and many nonprofit leaders still struggle to sustain their important missions. Like any business, nonprofits must compete – for resources, talent, attention – and that competition is relentless. At the heart of the leading from zero paradigm is the understanding that earning relevance to the marketplace happens one customer – and, in the case of the social sector, one constituent – at a time, and it cannot be taken for granted. This book outlines the important components that make up *Leading from Zero* and how leaders can put it into practice in their own organizations. Adding value, increasing efficiency, aligning to dynamic change, and embracing competition – these are the building blocks for great leadership in challenging times.

Anne Olin, President & CEO, nonprofit incubator Charitable Ventures

Dave Coffaro makes a very persuasive argument for adopting the mind-set of *Leading from Zero*. In the Age of Aquarius, the new normal is constant change and disruption. As a result, static systems or organizations that fail to learn nimbleness will fall to the wrong side of Schumpeter's Creative Destruction. If we've learned anything from the plague years we are currently experiencing, it is that tomorrow is not guaranteed, and the present doesn't look too stable either. Understanding the concept of "Flow" and leaning into a mind-set of adaptability and flexibility, while also having at core a set of principles that provide a firm foundation for one's "why" and a vision of where one is going are critical to surviving, and thriving, in the new perpetual state of change we find ourselves. In *Leading from Zero*, Dave helps leaders better understand how their roles must change to better enable their organizations to thrive in the new normal.

Don Perry, CEO, Digital Diaspora Family Reunion, LLC

Dave Coffaro's *Leading from Zero* not only hits the mark, but his timing is so relevant as we evolve from our worldwide crises to who knows what. He lays out the key steps to remaining relevant in an environment that seems to be moving faster than we can. What an excellent guideline on how to evolve in a world with too many soundbites. And he shares his guideline from every angle: customers, employees, and all stakeholders so that relevance permeates every intersection. Great and relevant read for today's world.

Kathy Bronstein, President KB Merchandising, Former CEO, Wet Seal, Inc.

In an era of remarkable change, this book provides a timeless template based on a novel adaptation of the zero-based budgeting approach. Nothing is guaranteed going forward. The past does not necessarily represent tomorrow. Focusing on solid principles to engage change rather than manage it, organizations can monitor and initiate actionable behaviors that lead to earned relevance by their customers, employees, and critical stakeholders. *Leading from Zero* skillfully vacillates between high level discussions on trending imperatives and firmly grounded operational recommendations. Chock full of historic and business examples, the reader uncovers the mindset and a paradigm that systematically enables organizations to dynamically respond to change.

Kevin J. O'Mara, Ph.D., CMA, Dean, Lundy-Fetterman School of Business, Campbell University

In *Leading from Zero*, David examines drivers that all organizations should be studying to stay relevant. David lays out a practical approach for examining those drivers to stay relevant. Multiple examples of real-world problems provide meaningful lessons when examined in context of how they impact relevance. For example, disruption is a driver all organizations need to keep on their radar through learning how to meet their clients' unrealized needs. In David's own words, writing the next chapter in your organization's story means unceasing re-definition of normal, enabling leaders to continually be on the lookout for cues and clues that will guide next steps – essential elements in *Leading from Zero*. Nice work David!

Janet D. Huber, Senior Vice President and Director of Inclusion, BOK Financial

Dave Coffaro's *Leading from Zero* gives structure and voice to the type of invaluable, hard-won lessons I learned while bootstrapping a new business. Surviving as a startup—striving for relevance while literally starting from zero—required analyzing the client experience in exacting detail, carefully allocating precious resources, and taking absolutely nothing for granted. Using a mix of big principles, tactical 'to dos' and compelling anecdotes, Dave creates a framework that would benefit leaders of other entrepreneurial ventures as well as much larger organizations—in short, insights for any leader with the confidence to embrace change and uncertainty and to continually assess their contract with both clients and employees.

David Lincoln, Partner, WISE

LEADING FROM

ZE
ro

Seven Essential Elements of Earning Relevance

David Coffaro

LEADING FROM ZERO

Seven Essential Elements of Earning Relevance

David Coffaro

Leading from Zero
Seven Essential Elements
of Earning Relevance

© 2021 David Coffaro
All Rights Reserved
Published by SACG United States

ISBN: **978-1-7344099-1-8**

Table of Contents

Foreword

Twenty years from now, some of the most recognized companies in the world will not exist. Household name brands will become footnotes in history. An Innosite study shows the 33-year average tenure of companies on the S&P 500 in 1964 fell to 24 years by 2016 and is forecast to shrink to just 12 years by 2027.

Many factors contribute to organizational longevity, perhaps none more than relevance with stakeholders: employees, customers, partners, and vendors. Earning and sustaining relevance - pertinence, meaningfulness, importance - is a leader's ongoing responsibility. Relevance decays when overlooked. Organizations that slip into irrelevance face the difficult task of re-earning standing with employees, customers, and other stakeholders, or riding a cycle of demise.

If you were asked names of companies you know that lost relevance, your list might include Toys "R" Us, Blockbuster, Payless Shoe Source, Palm, Compaq, Tower Records or Borders Books. You may identify manufacturers, wholesalers, restaurants, or businesses known only in your locale. In most examples on your list, relevance wasn't lost overnight. Some series of factors manifested themselves, company leaders missed or misread the environment, and failed to address diminishing relevance.

Losing relevance is unintentional. That is part of the problem - lack of intention to sustain relevance. Out of sight, out of mind. Leaders often keep long lists of important priorities yet overlook the essential elements of earning relevance. Sustaining relevance applies to for-profit and nonprofit organizations, and small, medium, and large enterprises across the globe.

How do organizations earn and sustain relevance?

One of the greatest responsibilities of leadership is driving continual evolution of the organization toward a well-defined future state. Without clear vision, businesses, processes, and leaders inevitably drift. Strategy defines the organization's vision from the current to a future state, from today's reality to aspirations for tomorrow. *Leading from Zero* defines, designs, refines, and delivers vision fulfillment through earning and sustaining relevance.

The purpose of this book: guide leaders in the practice of *Leading from Zero*. The formula is simple: vision, people, path, and relevance. Execution is more complex.

Vision – a picture of the organization's future state – is a thread pulled through *Leading from Zero* and a fundamental requirement of effective leadership.

Why focus on vision? An ancient proverb says vision without action is a daydream; action without vision is a nightmare. When organizations begin with a clear picture of their contribution to the world and why it matters, they establish a destination. Everything else follows vision - priorities, activities, processes, and results.

Absent a future state picture, organizations can be busy, engaged in urgent activities. Where will those activities lead? In the words of the Cheshire Cat in Alice in Wonderland, if you don't know where you want to go, it doesn't matter which path you take.

Organizational vision answers the question: What do we want our company to be? Vision guides priorities, activities and inspires engagement. It is aspirational and motivational. What a company does (mission), why they do it (purpose), and how they fulfill the mission (strategy) are informed by the vision.

It is said management is about finding answers; leadership is about asking questions. *Leading from Zero* asks: All things considered, how do we earn and sustain relevance with our stakeholders and fulfill our organization's vision?

As I work to earn and sustain relevance with my stakeholders, I am grateful to those who helped me in *Leading from Zero*. Carrie, Nicole, Michael, thank you for sharing ideas, tolerating my stories, and contributing solicited and unsolicited feedback. To my clients and colleagues – I am blessed through the rich lessons and opportunities you share daily. Lee Pound, thank you for your patience and attention to detail. Ron Riggio, you are a wonderful leadership and research mentor. Thank you for great inspiration. Dr. Jim Turrell, I am grateful for countless life lessons, inspiration, and guidance as my writing coach. Rob Kirby, you are an amazing, gifted artist and I'm grateful for your work and our friendship. James DaSilva, SmartBrief on Leadership, thank you for the opportunities to share new ideas through your publications. My deep gratitude to the business and academic leaders who generously invested time to review *Leading from Zero:* Kathy Bronstein, President KB Merchandising, Former CEO Wet Seal, Inc.; Janet Huber, Director of Inclusion, Bank of Oklahoma Financial; Kimberly Janson, PhD, CEO, Janson Associates; Kathleen Burns

Kingsbury, Founder, KBK Wealth Connection; Simone Lagomarsino, President & CEO, Luther Burbank Savings; David Lincoln, Co-founder/Partner, WISE; John Mattone, Founder & Co-Chairman, John Mattone Global, Inc.; Anne Olin, President & CEO, Charitable Ventures; Kevin O'Mara, PhD., Dean, Lundy-Fetterman School of Business, Campbell University; Don Perry, CEO, Digital Diaspora Family Reunion; Larry Tucker, Board Chair Emeritus, SCORE, and Ronald Riggio, PhD, Professor, Kravis Leadership Institute, Claremont McKenna College.

Introduction

A 1980s airline slogan said *we earn our wings every day*. The tagline means success is conditional, earned one experience at a time. The airline expanded on this slogan in print and television ads, saying all their employees were committed to working together, delivering on this promise through their activities every day. In television commercials gate agents, reservations representatives, ticket counter employees, ground support crew, flight attendants and pilots explained how they earned their wings. Every day started with a blank slate on which they created stories that defined the airline. Every day started at *zero*.

This positioning created implicit assumptions that every airline customer has a choice of providers; brand loyalty is limited; if we don't earn the right to serve a customer today, they'll chose another airline tomorrow. The day begins without customers.

Only through doing the right things to earn business do we move from zero customers to a thriving organization. Through every passenger interaction and flight, the airline's employees *earned the right to serve*, a meaningful, engaging esprit de corps.

A more familiar concept today, Zero-Based Budgeting, assumes each new budget cycle starts from a baseline of *zero* recurring revenue or expenses, no incremental expense increases over the prior period. Every dollar invested for existing or new activities stands on its own, justified in the current period, not the past. Zero-Based Budgeting assures manager accountability for revenue, expenses, and the activities they fund to create value in the organization.

Leading from Zero works on similar principles. Every organization starts its day from a base of *zero*. Zero customers. Zero employees. Zero revenue. Leaders must influence their organizations and *earn relevance* with customers, employees, and other stakeholders every day. Organizations have no entitlement to customers, employees, or revenue. Customers and employees have free will and only engage with an organization that demonstrates a relevant vision and clear value proposition and continually delivers on both. Obligations are temporary; contracts exist, but in the long run, all stakeholders (including vendors, contractors, suppliers, and investors) are free agents. For leaders, a fundamental question is, "How will I earn my relevance - earn my wings - today?"

These principles form a mindset from which leaders, starting at zero, must intentionally choose activities aligned with earning relevance among their stakeholders. When leaders take nothing for granted, they measure the value of each intentional activity by its alignment with the organization's vision. Through this mindset, leaders recognize accountability for assuring they continually uphold the vision as they influence activities intended to bring it to life, focus resources toward fulfilling the vision, and challenge any investments of time, attention or funds that diverge from the vision.

Leading from Zero principles are anchored in a set of assumptions:

- Competition for the highest value resources – human, physical, economic, non-economic – is constant.
- Barriers to entry in an industry are not permanent and the potential for new competitors is high.
- Competitive advantages are temporary at best.
- Constant pricing pressure results from the expectation that the company will provide more value to customers at lower prices.

These assumptions require a new strategic paradigm for the way in which leaders view their roles and build their organizations. This paradigm says an organization must:
- Recognize and align with the *dynamic nature* of its operating environment.
- Understand *resource development* as a differentiator.
- Practice *self-initiated disruption*.
- Exhibit a passion for *continually adding greater value*.
- Consistently demonstrate *efficiency gains* in operations.

Each element of this new paradigm represents an ongoing process, not a one-time event or special project. A *Leading from Zero* mindset informs the organization that effective execution of these processes earns relevance with employees, customers, and other stakeholders daily. Failure to re-earn relevance over time predisposes an organization to suboptimal access to the best resources, weakness relative to competition, and poor economic performance.

This failing also contributes to *vision drift* - losing sight of the future state, fragmenting attention, and distracting resources. Clarity and candor about *how* the organization's activities align with its vision avoids resource-draining diversions into products, projects, or ventures outside the company's core competencies.

In *How the Mighty Fall*, author Jim Collins describes the Undisciplined Pursuit of More as one of the Five Stages of Decline in a company. Collins wrote that companies in this stage, "Stray from the disciplined creativity that led them to greatness in the first place, making undisciplined leaps into areas where they cannot be great or growing faster than they can achieve with excellence, or both."

Leading from Zero requires the discipline to ask, "How are the activities my organization engages in today aligned with our vision, and how do they enable us to earn relevance with our employees, customers and stakeholders?"

Uncomfortable answers guide leaders to uprooting activities misaligned with the vision and deleterious to the organization's precious resources.

Leading from Zero distills this new strategic leadership paradigm into Seven Essential Elements of Earning Relevance:

- Leading by Cause
- Unceasing Re-definition of Normal
- Adaptive Disruption
- Process Mindset
- Seeing Your Organization as Others Do
- Winning Hearts and Minds
- Sustainability

These seven elements operationalize the paradigm within an organization. Each element anchors to the overriding theme of earning relevance every day. Employees, customers, and other stakeholders must receive value from the organization. If they don't, they'll part company to find it elsewhere. That's what happened with the airline that espoused earning their wings every day.

Eastern Airlines expressed the right idea with its motto. Founded in 1926, Eastern amalgamated smaller airlines acquired over decades to became one of the largest airlines in the United States. In the early 1980's, airline customers expectations changed. Airline operating costs rose. Deregulation changed the nature of competition, leading to the growth of no-frills airlines.

Eastern didn't adapt well to a new reality of their employees, customers, and suppliers. After a series of strategic missteps, they began to lose money. The company built a marketing campaign to differentiate itself with the focus on their service quality. Unfortunately, their actions didn't align with the concept of earning their wings every day. Eastern experienced safety issues, FAA fines, labor challenges, and a decline in passenger volume. In 1989 the company filed for bankruptcy and eventually sold off all assets.

A missed opportunity to *Lead from Zero*!

Chapter 1
The New Paradigm: Earning Relevance

When the year 2019 ended, the World Health Organization's (WHO) term - COVID-19, or coronavirus disease 2019 – did not yet exist. Not until New Year's Eve of that year did the WHO learn of the outbreak of a novel strain of coronavirus which caused severe illness. The coronavirus family of viruses were not new; researchers identified the first cases through upper respiratory tract infections in children in 1965. The severity was new.

Seventy-one days into the new year, the WHO labeled the newly discovered virus a pandemic. During that short time, the disease forced the world to shift from business as usual to navigating a new order of priorities, many of which were the antithesis of business as usual.

Global health immediately became *the* top priority. Making sure people avoided exposure to COVID-19 or recovered quickly became the number one focus for public and private sector organizations. Many business leaders experienced feelings analogous to operating at the base level of Maslow's Hierarchy of Needs. They began the year focused on self-actualization priorities. One survey[1] of business leaders published in January 2020 showed Leadership Development, Facilitating Employee Engagement, Improving Emotional Intelligence, Emphasizing Accountability, Leading Across Generations and Adding Diversity to the Leadership Team as top priorities for respondents' companies. All important; all higher-order priorities.

Suddenly, propelled by COVID-19, the conversation made a dramatic turn to a new focus on a different set of priorities – keeping people and organizations safe, delivering goods and services virtually where possible, managing the workforce remotely, and in certain cases, navigating a temporary suspension of some operations to keep the doors open, the business version of Maslow's baseline - food, water, shelter, and safety. This new, different world presented leaders with an ultimatum – *earn relevance or face obsolescence.*

The pandemic triggered a global reprioritization of activities. When the economy and many businesses paused, a *zero moment* emerged where customers didn't buy like before the event and employees' work changed, slowed, or stopped. Organizations went to zero. To regain relevance under those conditions, leaders took a strategic approach to harvesting new ideas to better position their organizations for an uncertain future, demonstrating the *Leading from Zero mindset.*

Systemic shock from the COVID-19 event created a forced zero moment unlike any socioeconomic event since the Second World War. All leaders of public and private sector organizations had to react. But what would a proactive approach to starting at zero look like?

---

[1] https://www.smartbrief.com/original/2020/01/2020-leadership-trends-industry-poll-interview

Starting the day at zero assumes yesterday's results do not predetermine today's experience. In the new paradigm, an organization must demonstrate *relevance* to employees, customers, shareholders, and other stakeholders to earn the right to serve. There are no guarantees yesterday's customers will continue their patronage, employees will return to work tomorrow, or vendors will continue their service. Past performance is not a foregone conclusion of future behavior.

A paradigm shift occurs when the accepted way of thinking – conventional wisdom - is replaced by a new and different approach. The *Leading from Zero* paradigm, operationalized through seven essential elements, holds earning relevance at its core. The *Leading from Zero* practice begins with a discussion about the new strategic paradigm imperatives.

Operating Environment Dynamic

Greek philosopher Heraclitus' statement, "Change is the only constant in life," is often cited as a reminder: When things finally settle down, something is likely to disrupt our comfort. We reach a steady state, change happens, then we're back to steady state. Reality is different; it is perpetual motion.

The business landscape is a dynamic environment in continuous change. In perceived steady state circumstances, we don't feel base-level change. Planet Earth moves at a speed of 1,000 miles per hour at the equator, yet we don't feel that base-level movement. Pandemics, economic and geopolitical ambulation accelerate and focus change to a perceptible level. Absent extraordinary accelerants, the nature of business *is* dynamic perpetual motion.

With sudden change accelerants, outdated, ineffective and misaligned operating models rise to the attention of leaders, employees, customers, and other stakeholders. Tuning into sub-surface level issues during base-level change is a *Leading from Zero* practice, comprised of three elements – recognition, alignment, and acuity.

> **Recognition** – Understanding change is an ongoing process, not a series of events.
>
> **Alignment** – Once perpetual motion is recognized, change is seen as an ongoing process, leaders align with flow instead of anchoring in events or static markers.
>
> **Acuity** – Aligned with the flow of change as an ongoing process, leaders proactively seek identification of operating models approaching inefficiency, offerings at risk of diminishing returns, and activities delivering decreasing value to the organization.

The pop music business is famous for producing one-hit wonders – performers that hit the charts with one song, never to be heard from again. The Kingsmen – *Louie Louie*, A-ha – *Take on Me*, The Knack – *My Sharona*, James Blunt – *You're Beautiful* are examples. The Rolling Stones are an exception. Formed in 1962 in London, the band has sold a quarter of a billion albums, earned three Grammy awards (from twelve nominations) released 30 studio albums, 30 live albums, 25 compilation albums and 121 singles. Fifty-eight years after their start, in July 2020, their song *Living in a Ghost Town* hit the #1 slot on the German singles chart (#3 on Billboard in the United States) making the Rolling Stones the oldest artists ever to reach number one.

Make no mistake – The Rolling Stones are a business, attuned to their operating environment dynamic. As customers' (music buyers) appetites changed, The Stones recognized shifts, aligned with the direction their audience evolved and demonstrated acuity in understanding how their operating model needed to evolve to earn relevance with their audience.

Consider their early music, emulating American blues artists. While Elvis blended gospel music with rhythm and blues, The Stones saw early indicators that something new – pop music – captured the attention of music buyers and added this new ingredient to their blues foundation. Their early recordings were in mono (the pre-stereo era), promoted through performances at small clubs and occasional appearance on BBC television.

As The Beatles created new paradigms expanding the definition of pop music, The Rolling Stones adjusted to the changing operating environment. Their music evolved, accompanied by shifts in production (in stereo, on singles, albums, eventually eight track and cassette tapes) and distribution (music shops, record stores, chain retailers, large outdoor concert venues with thousands of fans).

In a Wall Street Journal article titled *The Rolling Stones' Guide to Business Success,*[2] Rich Cohen described the band as "among the most dynamic, profitable and durable corporations in the world." Cohen describes a set of lessons for CEOs and entrepreneurs demonstrated by the band, two of which display earning, re-earning and sustaining relevance across stakeholders:

---

[2] https://www.wsj.com/articles/the-rolling-stones-guide-to-business-success-1462544656

Know what the market wants from you. By the time the Stones first single hit the market, the Beatles had positioned themselves as the cute, lovable, nonthreatening boys next door. The Stones needed to differentiate. In the words of guitarist Keith Richards, "So what does that leave us?" Instead of emulating the Beatles, as many other bands did, the Stones became their opposite: wholesomeness from the Beatles, raunchiness from the Stones. In the *Journal*, Cohen wrote, "They recognized a niche in the market and filled it."

Never stop reinventing. The Stones went through at least five stylistic iterations: cover band, '60s pop, '60s hard rock, '70s groove, '80s New Wave. Reinvention became the modus operandi for the Rolling Stones.

Disco, MTV, compact discs, digital recording, iTunes, YouTube, streaming music and video represent evidence of perpetual motion in the music business. The Rolling Stones recognized, aligned and adapted their operating model as the music business paradigm evolved. Every stop on their 2020 No Filter tour (canceled in March that year due to Covid-19) sold out within minutes or hours. Masterfully attuned to change as a process, the business known as The Rolling Stones understands what it takes to *Lead from Zero*, earning and sustaining relevance with their customers.

Resource Development as a Differentiator

I am a classic car enthusiast. My favorites are 1960's and 1970's American muscle cars and German roadsters. I love the design and details that define classic cars, particularly when restored to original condition.

Precise, authentic classic car restoration is an art and a science. It involves research into the vehicle's original condition specifications, accessing original equipment manufacturer parts and meticulous reconstruction. According to Classic Car Magazine,[3] there are four levels of automobile restoration:

- **Driver Level** – Good operating and body condition with the main purpose of providing the car's owner personal satisfaction.
- **Street Show Quality** - The car looks good and drives well. Most of the body work is of high quality. This level generally requires some professional craftsperson help with finer details of body restoration.
- **Show Cars** - These cars are restored with the intent of presenting at shows. Some restoration must be performed at the finest level of detail as professional judges will know the difference.
- **Concours** – Also known as mint condition, this level is for cars in national shows or private collectors who don't plan to drive the vehicle. The restoration process is defined by exemplary craftsmanship in developing the vehicle. The car is completely disassembled to prepare restoration. Significant research is performed to obtain original components, finishes and operating specifications, creating a flawless finished product.

These classic car restoration levels reflect a range of physical resource development, up to Concours condition, which

---

[3] https://classiccarmag.net/understanding-levels-of-car-restoration-and-costs-involved/

demonstrates an extraordinary commitment to vehicle advancement. A similar commitment is necessary to differentiate an organization as a *resource development exemplar*. *Stewardship* of human, physical, economic, and non-economic resources is to *acquisition* of these elements of capital as Concours is to Driver Level automobile restoration.

Organizations must make conscious decisions about their resource management philosophy. Options range from *threshold level* acquisition and application of resources to *exemplar level* of mindfully defined resource development protocols. At threshold level, the organization adds no value to managed resources. It simply engages or acquires then applies human, physical, economic, and non-economic resources to tasks.

Threshold level resource management often becomes evident in corporate acquisition strategies. The acquiring firm, which wants to expand existing business, merges with a competitor to access more customers, greater market share or enter new markets. This strategy often includes stripping out duplicative costs from the resulting merged organization with the rationale of creating more output with fewer net resources (eliminating positions, consolidating physical facilities, divesting duplicative functions). No investment is made in *developing* resources to further the company's vision. Simply adding resources of the acquired firm to the acquirer's inventory indicates threshold level strategy.

Note a distinction between cost cutting and efficiency gains. Efficiency gains emanate from efficient process redesign, elevated activity effectiveness and disciplined resource allocation. Mergers often present fertile ground for optimization of critical efficiency gains. Cost cutting in isolation is merely a mathematical exercise.

The distinction between threshold and exemplar level is how the company will care for resources. Human resource management strategy informs threshold vs. exemplar decisions. Today and into the foreseeable future, demographic trends and changes to the nature of work will increase demand for qualified talent. Workforce composition changes as older people work beyond traditional retirement age and population growth slows.

According to the U.S. Census Bureau's *Demographic Turning Points for the United States: Population Projections for 2020 to 2060*,[4] by 2030, one in five Americans will be at least 65 years old. Three years later, older adults are forecast to outnumber children (those younger than 18) for the first time in U.S. history. This trend is estimated to continue through 2060 when there will be 95 million older adults and 80 million children in the country.

This demographic evolution is expected to increase competition for human resources. At the same time, the nature of work is changing. Technology, applications of artificial intelligence, global supply chains and the need for continuous upskilling create complexities in effective human resource management. The need for technologically competent employees who adapt well to continuous change will shape demand for human resources.

In the context of these demographic changes and rising expectations of employees, leaders must address the question: Why would someone choose to work for our organization? *We*

---

[4] https://www.census.gov/content/dam/Census/library/publications/2020/demo/p25-1144.pdf

offer fair compensation and benefits is a threshold level response. An exemplar answer is based on commitment to ongoing development of talent and assumes employees value professional growth through knowledge and skill enhancement. The exemplar approach recognizes that people value working for organizations with a clear, authentic, and engaging vision that informs opportunities for doing meaningful work.

Why work for this organization? An exemplar might say: We recognize that success with customers is a result of our success in enabling and empowering team members to be the best they can be. Our team member development process is embedded in everything we do. Managers assure individual development plans are in place, followed and updated each quarter for every team member in the company. Manager compensation is linked to team member engagement scores. Becoming part of this organization is an opportunity to bring your experience to the team and grow to fulfill your highest professional goals.

Differentiation as a talent development exemplar is a well-thought-out strategy, implemented through engaged managers who understand the value of the human resources they steward. Soundbites saying "people matter here" or "people are our competitive advantage" are hollow unless they reflect the philosophy, strategy and actions aligned with nurturing and development of highly valued human resources. Mindful talent management strategy becomes a differentiator through a commitment to adding value to human resources under the organization's stewardship. Differentiation in this domain is essential to attract and retain the best available resources.

In the case of human resource management, a threshold level appears to be a contributing factor to employee disengagement and expensive, regrettable turnover. A Work Institute report[5] showed Career Development (opportunities for growth, achievement, and security) as the number one reason people leave their jobs for another organization. Further, this study suggests 77% of all employee attrition is "more preventable."

As a *Leading from Zero* paradigm imperative, the principle of differentiating an organization as a resource development exemplar applies to human, physical, economic, and non-economic resources available to the organization. Examples of other exemplary resource management strategies:

- *Physical Resources* - Residential, retail, and commercial property owner and management firm defines their target asset maintenance level as 97% - 100% flawless, meaning all safety standards are met or exceeded, no deferred maintenance, immediate repairs when issues arise, pristine landscaping and a consistent, high level of tenant satisfaction. The 2% margin serves to allow solutions that may require city or county permits or other delays in restoration to their standard that lay beyond their control.

- *Economic Resources* - Well capitalized regional commercial bank maintains credit underwriting and loan management standards that exceed regulatory

---

[5]https://cdn2.hubspot.net/hubfs/478187/2018%20Retention%20Report/Work%20Institute%202018%20Retention%20Report%20043018%20-%20Final.pdf?__hssc=163589856.1.1586381989873&__hstc=163589856.77ce7573404db301af742eeb001b83d5.1586381989872.1586381989872.1586381989872.1&__hsfp=786135133&hsCtaTracking=41368a2d-809b-4c8f-8e7a-e195fe5797b5%7C8141e251-f703-4a71-95f7-7cd1c49d7dce

requirements. As a result, loan to loss ratios fall below similar institutions and credit profit margins register top decile peer group performance.

- *Non-Economic Resources* – International entertainment and information company manages its brand as its most cherished asset, avoiding content, actions or investments which could jeopardize its reputation. The brand value carries over into demand for the company's products, ability to attract talent and a stock price premium.

- *Non-Economic Resources* – Nonprofit organization serving a county's homeless population practices a donor relationship management regime focused on donors' specific engagement interests in the mission. Major gift donors regularly participate in experiences which demonstrate transition from homelessness to full engagement in a productive life.

Exemplary resource development differentiates an organization, enhances its ability to attract the best available resources and demonstrates the *Leading from Zero* principle of continually earning relevance.

Self-Initiated Disruption

Al Zipf, a legend of the pre-digital banking era, is considered the father of electronic banking - the precursor to fintech (financial technology). In the early 1950s, Mr. Zipf developed the first large-scale, general purpose bank computing system at Bank of America. After that, he led a team that developed magnetic ink character recognition to encode and read data from checks, enabling processing automation. He earned several patents in the areas of banking technology, including a first-generation fax machine and the first-generation automated teller machine. Zipf, a master at self-initiated disruption, developed and implemented processes that saved time and money and enhanced the customer experience.

Most intriguing, colleagues described Mr. Zipf first and foremost as a *businessperson*. He surfaced business problems he could address with technology. Zipf approached self-initiated disruption to understand recognized and unrecognized needs, defined what the bank could do in-house and through third parties to address those needs, then delivered the goods. The key to Zipf's success came from starting with understanding the business and its customers, then defining how to use technology as his tool for initiating paradigm changing disruption.

Disruption happens. It's a natural force as industries evolve. Self-initiated disruption proactively identifies opportunities to create a paradigm shift benefiting an organization's (or industry's) stakeholders. Austrian economist Joseph Schumpeter used the term *creative destruction* to describe the way free markets evolve. In *Capitalism, Socialism, and Democracy*, Schumpeter wrote, "The opening up of new markets, foreign or domestic, and the organizational development from the craft shop to such concerns as U.S. Steel illustrate the same process of industrial mutation — if I may use that biological term — that incessantly revolutionizes the economic structure from within, incessantly destroying the old one, incessantly creating a new one."

Drawing from Schumpeter's words, self-initiated disruption revolutionizes an organization's value product (what it produces) from within, destroying the old one in favor of a new, more impactful value product.

Self-initiated disruption serves two purposes. First, it preempts external disruption by existing competitors and new entrants to your business. Second, it grounds the organization in its reason for existing through the employees, customers and stakeholders served.

This new paradigm holds that self-initiated disruption is an intentional strategy. Identification of opportunities for self-initiated disruption is a powerful tool for sustaining relevance. Preemptive and proactive, this strategy is fundamental to *Leading from Zero*. Use these four actionable steps in practicing this strategy:

- *Integrate Opportunity Identification into Regular Operating reviews* – Broaden standard quarterly financial performance reviews to include conversations about indicators of changing customer needs, preferences, trends, operational improvement opportunities, new technologies applicable to your business, new vendor practices and the like. This will identify seeds with potential to grow into full-blown paradigm shifts for your organization. Seek input broadly across the organization to hear ideas you may not have heard before.

- *Flash Insights* – Pay attention to transformational developments outside your industry that catch your attention as potentially applicable to your organization. Successful ideation is an iterative process, often stimulated through unrelated developments. In the 1930s, Kutol Products, a Cincinnati-based soap manufacturer, developed a product to clean coal residue from in-home fireplaces off wallpaper. Demand for the cleaner dropped following the introduction of vinyl wallpaper, which a sponge and water could clean. Kay Zufall, a nursery-school teacher, had a different idea on how to use the product. Zufall saw a newspaper article about making art projects with the wallpaper cleaning putty. She worked with the manufacturer to remove cleaning agents from the product, add coloring, and change the name from *Kutol's Rainbow Modeling Compound* to *Play-doh*.

- *Customer Listening Sessions* – Formal customer research is a valuable source of input. Informal customer listening sessions are potentially more powerful. Select a small group of five to ten customers to participate in a conversation with you to share what they like or don't care for from your organization, and what they seek elsewhere. In person is best. However, video listening sessions are highly impactful. Practicing the Art of Inquiry, listening with an open mind, never defending, and facilitating true conversation are essential elements of successful sessions.

- *Internal Startup Incubator* – Incubators exist to "incubate" new, disruptive ideas with the intention of developing a product, service, or business model. Creating this capability within your organization requires a clearly defined strategy and resource commitment. A benefit with this step is institutionalizing self-initiated disruption.

Passion for Continually Adding Greater Value

Maintaining status quo is not a viable option. Earning relevance, an ongoing process, is informed by dynamic expectations and circumstances. What met customers' expectations yesterday may fall short today. Leading a thriving organization requires the company continually identify new opportunities that will create more value for customers. Understanding what customers value and why, defining the connection as a *relationship* vs. *transaction*, and embedding these characteristics in business processes enables unbounded evolution of the organization.

In *Competitive Strategy*, Harvard professor Michael Porter described five forces that determine an industry's competitive intensity. The number and power of a company's competitive rivals, potential new market entrants, suppliers, customers, and substitute products define competitive intensity and impact a firm's profitability. These factors align with the importance of continually adding greater value for customers. More intense competition raises the bar for customer expectations. Still, each organization must choose to create greater value for its customers or react to competitive intensity.

Adding greater value requires defining dynamic objectives and metrics (how you measure value delivered to customers), then aligning these with individual employee expectations. Defining objectives is easier than measurement. Customer experience research provides quantitative insights into adding value. Research by the Medallia Institute shows that when companies provide a superior customer experience, financial performance improves. As a result, companies generate higher revenues (enhanced customer retention, greater purchase volume, upselling or cross-selling, and higher referral rates) and lower costs due to savings in customer acquisition and customer service.[6] While the total value of a great customer experience can be enormous, this study cautions it can also be difficult to quantify because often different departments and different financial statements capture its economic impact.

Notwithstanding measurement challenges, making a customer-based, customer-centric approach central to an organization's culture aligns with the principle of earning relevance. In her book *More is More*, customer experience author Blake Morgan says, "Customers do not come back just because you offer the cheapest product. They come back because you provide a superior product or service, and you do it in a way that makes their lives better and easier. Companies would benefit greatly from considering how every single decision affects the customer experience. Companies that understand the importance of a relationship are willing to go to any length to ensure that they continue to nurture the relationship. They do this through customer-focused strategies and leadership, via operations, policies, and procedures that consider how the customer will fare in every scenario."

To mean more than a marketing tagline, obsessing over creating greater value must become a cultural imperative and part of an organization's vision. A recent *Harvard Business Review* article by Denise Lee Yohn, *6 Ways to Build a Customer-Centric Culture* (HBR October 2, 2018), discussed the role of culture in consistently delivering to customers. Yohn wrote, "Perhaps the greatest barrier to customer centricity is the lack of a customer-centric organizational culture. At most companies, the culture remains product-focused or sales-

---

[6] https://go.medallia.com/rs/669-VLQ-276/images/Medallia-Accounting-for-a-Great-Customer-Experience.pdf

driven, or customer centricity is considered a priority only for certain functions such as marketing. To successfully implement a customer-centric strategy and operating model, a company must have a culture that aligns with these constructs, and leaders who deliberately cultivate the necessary mindset and values in their employees."

Leading from Zero requires focused curiosity about what matters to customers, understanding and anticipating needs and delivering in better, simpler ways. Living this principle requires comfort navigating continuous evolution of a business.

Stability comes not from a status quo, rather from anchoring in a vision which defines the endgame for all activities in the organization. *Normal* is dynamic, not static. Ironically, what we may have perceived as a *normal* competitive environment in the past was a point on a continuum of change to which we became accustomed. The perennial question for leaders is – *what comes next*?

Consistently Demonstrating Efficiency Gains

As part of a strategy project I led with a nonprofit organization, I took the operations team to tour a large food company's regional distribution center. The company we visited supplies large and mid-sized restaurant and retail chains internationally. We took the tour to identify the best practice ideas of that for-profit enterprise that we could transfer to the nonprofit.

The food company, in its seventh decade of operation, showed no signs of resting on their laurels. The company continually reviewed every activity – receiving and inventorying incoming product, moving pallets to their proper storage location, order fulfilment, loading pallets to fill delivery trucks and transportation logistics – to identify a faster, more efficient, safer, and less expensive approach. Every work shift started with a brief meeting to assure a focus on safety and effectiveness. Transportation logistics evaluated weather, traffic conditions, fuel prices and vehicle conditions to assure optimal efficiency in delivering food and supplies to customers.

The company measured, monitored, reviewed, and refined all processes in their search for efficiency gains. Most processes we observed on our tour were implemented within the previous 24 months because they evolved through continuous process improvement. Within 24 months following our tour, most processes would be redesigned again as part of the company's business as usual search for efficiency gains.

That food company exemplifies the principle of consistently demonstrating efficiency gains across the organization. The company created results from efficient process redesign, elevated activity effectiveness and disciplined resource allocation – cultural characteristics informing unyielding attention to continuous improvement.

Efficiency gains, small or large, result from consistency of focus. This principle contrasts with transformational change efforts, which are designed to move the organization from its current state to a new, different future state. Transformational change events stem from a root cause like evolution in the competitive environment, cost pressure, pricing compression, implementation of new technology, or a new regulatory framework.

This element of earning relevance serves two purposes. First, efficiency across the organization benefits customers through the value they experience from products, services, and access to what they need. Second, consistently generated efficiency gains produce economic benefit to customers (in the form of pricing), employees (learning, upskilling, career pathing) and owners (profits). Ongoing, incremental efficiency gains are business as usual in *Leading from Zero*.

The *Leading from Zero* paradigm provides a framework and actionable principles, further distilled into the *Seven Essential Elements of Earning Relevance*.

Chapter 2
Leading by Cause

Balancing resolve for relevance with results

In 1989, Donald Messersmith, an entomologist at the University of Maryland, participated in a project initiated by the U.S. National Park Service to address concerns about deterioration of two national monuments – the Lincoln and Jefferson memorials in Washington, D.C. An associated Press story reported these memorials were slowly crumbling under the ravaging effects of water seepage, air pollution, littering tourists, and a pesky little bug called the midge.[7]

As an insect expert, Professor Messersmith's job included understanding why the midges flocked to these monuments and how these bugs impacted the structures. Messersmith's analysis of the situation found that in the springtime, as dusk turns to evening, midges arise from the Potomac River, where they've spent the winter as larvae in the mud. By the millions, the midges flock to the bright lights of the nearby Lincoln and the Jefferson memorials. Midges lay eggs on the walls, leave droppings, or simply die there. Midge remnants attract hungry

---

[7]

https://news.google.com/newspapers?nid=1345&dat=19900417&id=NXZMAAA
AIBAJ&sjid=BfoDAAAAIBAJ&pg=6930,2227469

spiders who come to eat, then spin webs in cracks in the mortar. And the spiders leave droppings, too. The spiders attract local birds who come to eat and leave their droppings while they are at the monuments. To clean the abundance of bird droppings, maintenance people frequently perform pressure washings using harsh chemicals, which contribute to deterioration of the Lincoln and Jefferson memorials.

Messersmith concluded the root cause underlying accelerating deterioration of the monuments was their lighting. By delaying lights coming on at dusk when midges are active, the insects would find another place to go. Absence of midges would keep spiders away, and with no spiders, birds would be forced to find food elsewhere. Less mess to clean means fewer chemical-heavy washings and reduced wear and tear on the memorials.

Professor Messersmith's project is often used to illustrate *root cause analysis*. The effect in this case: two aging Washington D.C. monuments deteriorated at an accelerating rate. On the surface, the cause appeared to be the use of harsh chemicals in cleaning monuments. The lesson is designed to encourage learners to go below the surface and ask: Why are harsh chemicals used? The answer: To remove the large number of bird droppings on the monuments. Why are there so many bird droppings on these monuments? Answer: Birds are attracted to the spiders on the monuments. Why there so many spiders on and around the monuments? Answer: Spiders feed on the midges that nest on the monuments. Finally, why are there so many midges on the monuments? Answer: Lighting of the monument in the evening acts like a magnet, attracting midges.

By getting to the root cause of the problem, the right set of actions can be implemented to change the effect. In this case,

Messersmith suggested the solution: Change when lighting is turned on in the evening. By delaying onset of monument lighting, Messersmith surmised midges would find another place to go, thus the series of events causing accelerating deterioration would change, slowing the deleterious impact of frequent cleaning.

For the record, the National Park Service performed a six-week pilot program in 1990. Lights around the monuments were delayed until one hour after sunset on three days a week. Professor Messersmith and his team tracked the number of midges on the monuments nights when lights were delayed by an hour, compared with those evenings where lights came on at dusk. By the completion of the pilot, Messersmith documented an 85% reduction in midge infestation.

For our purposes, the learning from this case is the practice of deconstructing results as thoroughly as possible to determine *the* root cause of results. *Leading from Zero* is about earning, re-earning, and sustaining relevance with stakeholders daily, which requires a clear understanding of results; why a strategy works or falls short of producing expected results. Even with multiple contributing factors (chemical washing, birds and bird droppings, spiders, and midges in this example), results deconstruction leads to a single thread responsible for connecting each element in the story.

Below the surface

Understanding root cause is logical. Some combination of activities and circumstances created results. Yet, business leaders train to focus on results. Know your numbers, make your numbers, and if things fall short, do more to make plan.

Early in my career, a manager said, "We pay for results in this company. Get the results or we'll find someone who will."

A better message: "Whatever results you create, let's understand activities contributing to the outcomes, whether they are on plan, better, or worse than expected. When results meet expectations, we know what to continue; when they don't, we can determine what needs to change to create what we expect." Looking below the surface leads to deeper understanding and new ideas to fulfil the organization's vision.

When we use the term *just the tip of the iceberg* to describe a situation, we mean evidence we see is part of a larger or more complex issue, with more causal information below the surface. The tip of the iceberg idiom is often attributed to the Titanic story. Tragic consequences resulted from the misjudgment by Titanic's captain, Edward John Smith, on April 14, 1912. While the crew had received several warnings of ice in the Titanic's path off the coast of Newfoundland, Captain Smith chose to maintain the ship's speed at 22 knots. The exact size of the iceberg struck by the Titanic is unknown, but recent computer modeling estimates its total size at 75 million tons, or 1442 times the size of the ship. While evidence of the iceberg projected above the ocean surface, its submerged body was exponentially larger.

Organizational issues impacting employees, customers and other stakeholders often reside deep below surface-level appearances, portending substantive risks to the company's relevance. Wells Fargo opening accounts without customer permission surfaced a deeper-rooted issue with branch employee performance measurement and production expectations. Chipotle's 2015 e-coli issues surfaced structural supply chain and proper food handling issues. Two Boeing 737

Max crashes brought to light unfeasible production and delivery assumptions rooted in deeper cultural concerns. In each case, management had the opportunity to *Lead by Cause* by deconstructing results and addressing source issues before experiencing crises of relevance.

Tom and Mike cofounded a window covering business, providing in-home sales and installation of custom, mid-priced to high-end blinds, shutters, and drapes. They operated in an affluent Southern California suburban market, where new home, town house and condominium construction was strong. Their business took off like a rocket, with sales doubling every quarter. Tom and Mike were great working with clients, understanding their practical needs and aesthetic preferences and exceeding expectations. To keep up with growth, they added staff, expanded their serving area, and caught the attention of local business media impressed with their rapid growth.

I came into the picture as a consultant toward the end of the company's seventh year. Tom and Mike made the decision to franchise their window covering business as a strategy for fueling national growth. By the time my engagement began, the company had grown to 125 franchisees in 20 states, a handful of company-owned territories and a headquarters staff built to run the business. One of the biggest issues was understanding what business they were in.

The company's business attorney, concerned about declining revenues, lack of strategic focus and growing dissatisfaction among franchisees, referred Tom to me. On the surface, these real issues required immediate attention. Mike left the company a year earlier due to conflicts. Tom decided his franchisees were the main issue. If the company recruited more superstar operators, things would turn around. In fact, the issues described by Tom and his attorney were simply the tip of the iceberg.

Results deconstruction uncovered a series of underlying issues stemming from misunderstanding of this company's business drivers. In the beginning, Tom and Mike were in the window covering business. Selling and installing window coverings was the way they delivered value to their customers and the source of their revenue. With 125 franchisees, the largest revenue source came from franchise fees. When franchisees were successful, the franchisor generated revenue in the form of a 10% royalty fee on all window covering sales.

The nature of the business as a franchisor shifted to franchisee enablement. Tom's mission needed to center on effective, consistent execution of a clear operating model through each franchisee. That meant understanding the root causes of franchisee success, distilling causes into actionable, repeatable elements, and transferring that knowledge to franchisees for application in their daily activities. It meant creating an easy-to-follow operating process and manual, model training, franchisee development, brand development, brand marketing, and national sales support. It meant Tom's role as CEO translated into creating an environment that made it easy for franchisees to succeed.

Franchisee dissatisfaction came from feeling they were on their own, with no support in operating their business. In most cases, franchise operators were previously employees working in businesses other than window coverings. Few had experience running their own business. When they signed on to become a window covering franchisee, they expected to receive step-by-step guidance on how to run a business. They wanted to follow an instruction manual that addressed every step in the process, from how to get a business license to processing payments for sales completed.

As we worked through identifying root causes of operating results, and developed a strategic plan for the company turnaround, Tom recognized that the role he needed to play wasn't the role he wanted to play. He loved working directly with customers, using his creativity to impact a home's interior design. He wasn't excited about engaging in activities necessary for success in leading a large group of franchisees. Eventually, Tom sold the company.

Leading by Cause draws a leader's attention below surface-level evidence to understand origin and dimension of what manifests as a result. Lessons throughout history inform us that cause precedes effect; actions create results. Plato explained the principle of causality, saying, "Everything that becomes or changes must do so owing to some cause; for nothing can come to be without a cause." (Timaeus 28a).

In Codex Atlanticus, Leonardo DaVinci wrote, "No effect is in Nature without cause; you understand the cause and you do not need any experience."

As every school child learns, for every action, there is an equal and opposite reaction per Sir Isaac Newton's third law.

With depth of affirmation around cause preceding effect, why do business leaders focus so heavily on analyzing their numbers or focus on the effect instead of the cause? A recent conversation with a community bank CEO focused on his vision for the company. He opened the dialog saying he and his leadership team had put a lot of thought into where they wanted to take their bank, and they committed to a *vision* to deliver top decile ROE, ROA and topline revenue growth. A quintessential example of focusing on effect, not cause. At no point in our conversation did he mention activities the bank would focus on to create these results (i.e., expanding client relationships, adding new services, applying new technology to enhance ease of doing business, developing new client relationships, lowering operating costs).

In their *CFO Magazine* article, *How An Obsession with Metrics Is Killing Your Company,*[8] authors Alexander Van Caeneghem and Jean-Marie Bequevort write, "The quest for financial performance and the pressure to measure can corrode organizational cultures, narrow the focus of leadership, reduce intrinsic motivation, and support unethical behavior."

With a similar theme, Michael Harris and Bill Taylor's *Harvard Business Review* article, *Don't Let Metrics Undermine Your Business,*[9] said "A company can easily lose sight of its strategy and instead focus strictly on the metrics that are meant to *represent* it."

We can *manage* cause, but only *measure* effect. Yet we often overlook the real story - the aggregation of activities that *created* results reflected in our numbers. *Leading by Cause* is an approach that says we use *results* to understand activities, effectiveness, and efficiency in context of the organization's vision and strategy. When results do not meet expectations, the root cause is embedded in one (or more) of these elements: choices of activities performed, performance effectiveness, and performance efficiency. Shifting to cause-based analysis of results positions leaders to laser-target interventions like

---

[8] https://www.cfo.com/analytics/2016/04/obsession-metrics-killing-company/
[9] https://hbr.org/2019/09/dont-let-metrics-undermine-your-business

coaching, guiding, managing, or taking direct action to change the trajectory of outcomes. There are three paradoxes to navigate in making the shift to *Leading by Cause*:

- **Effect vs. Cause Conversations:** Cause-based performance analysis requires understanding the composition of activities that created results. A common effect-based conversation among managers when results don't meet expectations starts out with, "Revenue is 5% below target, so let's do everything we can to drive it up and make plan." A cause-based conversation gets at the root, "What were the sales activities last month that created these results? Which customers did we focus on? How did we engage those customers? How did they react to what we have to offer? Are we able to identify any changes in customer preferences or expectations? What is getting in the way of our new business development activities? What has changed in the competitive environment?"

- **Appearance of Improvement vs. Improvement:** In the effects domain, managers often look for steps to improve the appearance of P&L results, yet no real underlying change takes place. For example, they delay travel or defer other expenses in the last weeks of a quarter to create the appearance of lower operating costs, thus a better bottom line. Results may look good, but the root cause creating undesirable results has not been sleuthed out.

- **Math vs. Behavior:** Operating results presented in an organization's P&L reflect aggregation of activities. It is easy to analyze operating results in a sterile manner, quantifying month-over-month changes and variance to plan. Of course, numbers don't lie! But every numeric result – sales, revenue, expenses, product development, marketing, manufacturing, and distribution – reflects human behavior. Cause-based analysis of results seeks to understand the behavioral factors contributing to outcomes reflected on the P&L. Conversation starting questions might be: *What changed in our business development activities last quarter vs. the same period last year? What effect is our largest competitor's new delivery strategy having on our sales?* or *How effective is the collaboration between product management, manufacturing, and sales?* This line of inquiry takes leaders below the surface and into the domain of results origins; that is the place where activity adjustments can be made to create better results.

Getting at root cause also helps avoid under-estimating or over-simplifying what it takes to create better outcomes. The Dunning-Kruger effect is a cognitive bias in which people overestimate their knowledge or ability in certain areas, often underestimating the complexity of a problem. This effect can occur when a lack of self-awareness prevents one from accurately assessing their own skills and underlying causes of the issue. *Leading by Cause* requires deconstruction of results into elements, identifying origin of activities which created results, then determining where and how adjustments will be made going forward to change outcomes. Understanding results is important; knowing what *caused* them and what intervention will create better results is empowering.

Chapter 3
Unceasing Re-definition of Normal

Does status quo exist? The term refers to normalcy in the current state-of-affairs. Ironically, what we perceive as *normal* is simply a point on a continuum of change to which we become accustomed Normal is dynamic, like watching a child grow. She looks the same when you see her every day, then suddenly she's grown.

Her growth didn't happen in an instant; it occurred through a process of development. In operating environments, movement is continuous, albeit at varying speeds. Systemic shocks can substantially accelerate the rate of change. Other environments can create the appearance of constancy.

The largest retail chain in the United States in 1970 represented 1% of the country's entire economy. Two-thirds of Americans shopped there. Half the country's households had the retailer's credit card. Business analysts considered the company the core to the fabric of the country. Over the next five decades, Sears continually missed opportunities to re-earn its relevance in the eyes of the company's customers.

Richard Sears, a railroad agent in North Redwood, Minnesota in the late 1800's, built a side business, selling watches through mail order. As his watch business grew, Sears developed a partnership with Alvah Roebuck, a watch repairman. In 1887, Sears published his first mail order catalog selling watches, diamonds, and jewelry. Six years later, the partners renamed the company, now based in Chicago, Sears, Roebuck and Co. Its mail order catalog expanded to include product lines beyond watches and jewelry.

Sears understood that their customers, primarily rural farmers, wanted access to a wider range of products at better prices than they could find through small town general stores. The company earned relevance by offering products their customers needed through the catalog. By 1895, the Sears catalog had evolved to 532 pages of home and farm supplies, sewing machines, bicycles, sporting goods, appliances, toys and groceries.

As customers and communities changed and more Americans settled in urban centers, the company practiced initiating self-disruption to re-earn relevance. In 1925, at the risk of cannibalizing its catalog-only business, Sears opened its first retail stores just as America evolved into a mobile society. Sears designed its retailing model to align with new practices. Store product mix, design and locations considered the needs of men and women customers shopping without the assistance of a salesperson. Following World War II, Sears embarked on an aggressive expansion plan, added stores in suburban markets and in the West while sustaining its catalog distribution channel.

At its peak in the late 1960's, Sears' owned an iconic brand, but company leadership drifted away from their customers new normal, an emerging trend that Sears leaders didn't acknowledge.

In his Fortune magazine article, *Sears' Seven Decades of Self-Destruction*, author Geoff Colvin chronicled leadership's pattern of overlooking new normal stages as they unfolded. He wrote, "The company grew, the stock boomed. But the world changed, and Sears leaders didn't see, perhaps didn't want to see, that their business model — based on broad selection, high service, and periodic steep-discount sales — was becoming an antique."

Colvin added, "Retail consumers were enthusiastically embracing a new way of buying: the discount store, built on low prices, minimal service, and high merchandise turnover. In 1962, a miracle year for retailing, Walmart, Kmart, and Target all opened their doors. Sears leaders were aware of the phenomenon but felt serenely unthreatened. They seemed not to grasp that they faced a fundamentally different new breed which offered much lower prices in relatively bare-bones settings. But customers noticed the difference."

A new normal emerged. That new normal led to another, and another. What Sears overlooked, Walmart, Target and eventually Amazon seized upon. *Leading from Zero* requires an unceasing re-definition of normal; recognizing when a new phase of normal begins, addressing the changes and knowing the company is traversing a process point, not a destination.

The Problem with Believing Your Own Press

At one point in her career, my mother worked as a public relations manager for United California Bank in Los Angeles. After college, she became a newspaper editor, where she learned the importance of storytelling and its connection with developing effective public relations strategies. One of her adages was *never believe your own press*. The principle: when a company or individual receives favorable press coverage, they can lose sight of reality and become hypnotized into believing their own headlines. It turns out that mom's advice is supported with research.

A study performed by Matthew Hayward, Violina Rindova and Timothy Pollock at University of Colorado, Boulder,[10] explored strategic implications of CEO celebrity for the future actions of the CEO and her firm. Their analysis drew on social cognition and decision-making research to explore how celebrity affects the CEO's self-impression of who she is and her capabilities. If celebrity arises from the over-attribution of outcomes to dispositional, versus situational factors, a CEO who believes her own press is likely to become overconfident about her abilities and the accuracy of her judgment and more committed to the strategic choices that made her a celebrity. As a result, her firm may over rely on the strategic actions that brought her celebrity in the first place and become less adaptable to new competitive demands. Hubris arises when CEO overconfidence results in problematic decisions, including undue persistence with actions that produce celebrity.

Robert was division manager of a national bank. He was hired to his position based on his work as a consultant to the bank. Although Robert didn't have banking experience, he was a quick study and demonstrated his intellectual and problem-solving abilities throughout a complex consulting engagement with the firm. The manager who hired Robert believed by hiring the smartest people available, he would create the best

---

[10] http://www.timothypollock.com/pdfs/smj04-celebrity.pdf

leadership team in the business. Robert was onboarded with great fanfare and high expectations for what he could achieve leading this division.

I began working with Robert when he was one year into his division manager role with the bank. Like his manager, I too was impressed with Robert's intelligence and analytical acumen. In a short time, he had developed broad knowledge of the business and its economic drivers. Conversely, part of my assignment was to help Robert turn things around. He entered his role as a welcome superhero; within eighteen months, he was perceived as out-of-touch and at risk of termination.

Robert was hired to move an outdated, ineffective business model forward, aligned with current client expectations. Intellectually, he understood his assignment. What his manager failed to recognize prior to hiring Robert was his lack of patience and discomfort listening to input from his key stakeholders (clients, colleagues, employees).

Robert's success as a consultant came from analyzing data fed to him from his clients. Reacting to data received led Robert to conclusions limited to those specific data. Real-world problems are identified and addressed through disciplined broad-based inquiry, collaborative ideation, developing new strategies aligned with the business's vision and engaging team members across an organization in co-owning the plan. Plan execution is subject to evolution as evidence from unceasing re-definition of normal unfolds. Robert was unwilling to adjust his approach, leading him to exit his position with the bank.

Research, Robert's story, and the Sears case highlight a set of factors which contribute to overlooking strategic implications of a continually unfolding new normal. The

Leading from Zero philosophy offers mitigants to reduce the risk of each factor.

Legacy Fallacy

This factor is defined by reliance on the view that what got us here will get us to the future. Competencies matter, but they do not operate in isolation. Leaders walk a fine line of balancing building upon legacy success factors and overreliance on yesterday's success formula.

Mitigants
- Anchor in an appreciation for the organization's history without attachment to the way we've always done things.
- Recognize that an operating playbook is only applicable to a specific set of circumstances; when circumstances change, the playbook requires refinement.
- Continuous fine-tuning of the organization's vision, priorities, and activities as new phases of normal unfold is necessary to carry a successful organization into its future state.

Denial of Imminent Change Indicators

The perspective that current results, performance, customer behavior, or competitive changes are simply anomalies enables a narrative where leaders wait until things get back to normal before digging deeper into root cause. The longer changing conditions are rationalized as anomalies, the greater the risk to the organization.

Mitigants

- Implement an operating agreement co-owned by all team members requiring review of performance variances by a peer in another area of the business. The peer review purpose is to generate questions and observations that shine a light on imminent change unintentionally rationalized by team members closest to the circumstances.

- Include dedicated time in regular business operating reviews to explore new, emerging, or potential trends external to the organization. This includes new market research, competitor actions, industry analyses and team members' observations. This committed time allows operating managers to shift attention from current reality to environmental factors they might otherwise overlook or deny.

Unconventional Wisdom

We engage in the perception that because we think differently, we must be right. In his book *What Got You Here Won't Get You There*, leadership author Marshall Goldsmith says, "People who think they can do no wrong usually can't admit they are ever wrong, which, paradoxically, makes you more wrong." At an organizational level, this factor inhibits leaders' ability to see emerging changes in their operating environment until it's too late to perform as a first responder in the next new normal.

Mitigants

- Recognize while contrarian views can have value, different isn't always better.

- Ask yourself and your colleagues, *What is the substance supporting our position on this issue*? If the answer sounds like rationalizing difference for the sake of difference, examine the position and determine how it aligns with the organization's vision, priorities, and objectives, in context of an evolving next new normal.

Fear of Change

It is real, yet infrequently articulated or properly addressed in organizations. Gustavo Razzetti, author of *The Adaptive Mind* column in *Psychology Today,* said, "We fear change because we can't anticipate the outcome. However, staying put can be riskier than changing. The paradox is that although we reject uncertainty, we have the skills to change and evolve. Fear is an emotion that gets in the way. Our brains prefer a predictable, negative outcome over an uncertain one. On the other hand, our mind is flexible and adaptive — it can be trained to thrive in change."[11]

When the rate of change in our business environment accelerates, uncertainty increases. Until an organization surfaces concerns for exploration, discussion and resolution, fear of change will influence action or inaction.

Mitigants
- Acknowledge that a new paradigm is unfolding and recognize there is uncertainty about the future.
- Recognize any fear you, your team members, or others in the organization may be feeling.

---

[11] https://www.psychologytoday.com/us/blog/the-adaptive-mind/201809/how-overcome-the-fear-change

- Define what you expect of yourself and your team members in navigating the next new normal.
- Focus on what the organization can control.
- Communicate all you can about the emerging next new normal and how your organization plans to navigate the environment.

Bureaucratic Inertia

This shows up in comments like, "If only we could get out of own way, we could tackle what needs to change." The relationship between a tendency to do nothing or remain unchanged (inertia) and engaging in addressing barriers to evolution (bureaucracy) is that both conditions manifest as inaction, creating deleterious outcomes in a rapidly changing environment. Risk arises from the length of time and energy it takes just to get ready to deal with an emerging new normal.

Mitigants
- Acknowledge that the past is not a perfect predictor of the future. Consequently, previous experiences of bureaucratic inertia do not mandate a repeat performance; people and organizations have a tremendous innate ability to adapt to changing conditions, and leaders set the tone for agility.
- Recognize a changing environment *will* impact your organization, and proactive engagement in the transition to the next new normal creates greater freedom to choose your path forward.

Comfortable (Critical) Mass Mindset

This experience looks like Bureaucratic Inertia, but the root cause is a level of comfort with the way things are that interferes with the organization's drive to consider the next new normal until change cannot be avoided. The critical mass element implies that comfort with current reality is broad based.

When I was a kid, my dad drove an American Motors Rambler. I never understood why he would choose to drive that incredibly square vehicle when there were Mustangs and Camaros on the market. My mom, less concerned with the lack of cool the Rambler represented, laser-focused on its mechanical problems. I recall two events when the Rambler broke down as dad drove our family home late at night.

After the first episode, mom encouraged dad to trade in the Rambler on a used Chevy or Ford that would be more reliable. But dad liked his car. However, he did agree to think about making a change. After the second late night stall-out, mom made it clear that *thinking* about trading in the Rambler was no longer an option. The next weekend, dad accepted that he needed to move from his comfort zone and get rid of his old Rambler.

The good news was that decided to act and replace his car. At five years old, I loved cars, so dad invited me to go with him to shop for a replacement car. On his way to the Chevrolet dealership, he drove past the American Motors used car lot. Bad news! They had a big month-end sale taking place, and a newer version of dad's Rambler American sat on display on a grandstand in front of the dealership. Dad stopped in to look.

I remember the salesman telling my dad, "I'm not going to let you leave here tonight without the car of your dreams."

The price was right, and they even took the older model Rambler as a trade-in. Dad was excited about his purchase for the entire drive home. On the other hand, when we pulled into the driveway, mom greeted us. She wasn't pleased with the decision. Six months later, mom drove dad to the Chevy dealership where they traded in the second Rambler for a three-year-old Caprice.

Mitigants

- Recognize businesses operate in a dynamic environment, always in motion.
- Understand that today's organizational comfort zones become uncomfortable quickly as a new operating environment unfolds.
- Acknowledge that the discomfort associated with moving away from current comfort is less than adapting to change forced upon the organization.
- Identify opportunities to leverage organizational competencies leaning into new realities presenting themselves in the business environment.

Unceasing Re-definition of Normal Begins with Vision

The question for leaders is – given the dynamic nature of our operating environment, *what comes next for this organization*? The *next phase of normal* is a continually evolving story for each organization to write. An economy or industry is an aggregation of individual and organizational actions aligned with some set of objectives. Following systemic shocks, industry disruption or evolution, companies tend to wait until after the dust settles to interpret the environment, then take actions toward a next new normal. An alternative, the *Leading from Zero* approach, is to begin defining your organization's next phase of normal when imminence of change becomes apparent.

One of the greatest responsibilities of leadership is *driving continual evolution of the organization* toward a well-defined future state. Context for the organization's future state vision is the environment in which it operates. Vision connects *what* an organization does to the external world. As that environment changes, leaders must ask – all things considered, including our new normal, does our future state vision still fit the environment?

Everything a leader does must be aligned with the vision. Without a clear vision, organizations, processes, and leaders inevitably drift from their goals. This principle applies even in a fast-moving environment, where stability is achieved through anchoring to the guiding vision. As the operating environment changes, sustaining a focus on what your company does (mission), why you do it (purpose), and how you fulfill your mission (strategy) leads to greater organizational stability. With a clear vision, organizations can find comfort in uncertainty and stability in progress. Vision is a state of being that an organization expects to create and informs priorities which distill into activities. Vision, priorities, and activities must be aligned to create the results the organization expects. Core competencies put a fine point on the organization's vision and provide clarity about day-to-day activities.

In early 2000, an epic merger took place between two companies from different worlds. The deal, valued at $165 billion, was the largest in history at that time. The resulting company – AOL Time Warner - became the world's largest media conglomerate. America Online, a new world media company, played a lead role in the emerging internet arena, delivering dial-up internet access, web browser capability and email. Time Warner, a legacy media organization, had deep roots in entertainment, film, music, and print.

It didn't take long for issues to arise as the companies came together. Early on, culture clashes between the two companies became evident. Steve Case, founder and CEO of AOL, left the board of the combined company in 2005, declaring the merger a failure. Soon after his departure, Case said, "Vision without execution is hallucination. Having a good idea is important but being able to execute the idea is even more important, and that comes down to people and priorities, and we were unable with the combined AOL Time Warner company to get that side of it right."[12]

Leading from Zero recognizes vision fulfillment takes place through people, guided by priorities - priorities informed by well-defined understanding of continually evolving normal. Here are four ideas on how to begin defining your organization's next phase of normal as indicators point to the imminence of change:

- ***Recast a Rolling Quarterly Strategic Plan*** – Operating plans established at the beginning of a fiscal year can become obsolete as new phases of normal unfold. As you develop a definition of new normal, take a strategic approach to recasting plans beginning by revisiting the organization's vision. With a clear picture of the future

---

[12] https://www.businessinsider.com/steve-case-lesson-aol-time-warner-merger-2018-10

state in context of the new normal, deconstruct that vision into a new set of priorities and specific activities that will bring the future state to life. I recommend distilling priorities into a rolling set of six quarterly milestones, adjusting expectations and metrics every 90 days. This enables organizational agility as the next, and subsequent, stages of new normal unfold. Capitalize on the fact that every 90 days, the operating environment for the next quarter becomes clearer.

- *Intentional Discontinuation* – In the world of art, the concept of negative space describes area around the subject, or areas of interest. As a docent at the Chicago Museum of Art explained, *negative space is everything the sculptor chips away from a block of marble when creating a statue.* The corollary in defining the next new normal for an organization is stripping away anything that is not of value in the future state. Michael Porter said, "The essence of strategy is choosing what not to do." As a new normal unfolds, this means identifying activities, processes, products, or services that no longer serve the organization as targets for elimination. By exploring questions about which activities have outlived their usefulness, leaders can free-up capacity to apply more impactfully in the next new normal.

- *New Offerings* – What new needs has your organization observed with your customers as indicators of a new normal surface? Throughout history, new ideas and offerings have emerged from extraordinary environments. During World War I, to help soldiers avoid being distracted by their pocket watches, manufacturers began attaching straps to the watch faces they produced. The idea wasn't new, but demand for wearable timepieces grew significantly following the war, allowing forward-thinking manufacturers a meaningful long-term growth opportunity.

- *Development Opportunities* – During the COVID-19 event, leaders learned about efficacy of their business continuation plans during the crisis phase. They also observed strengths and developmental needs of team members and the organization overall as the nature of customer engagement and operations quickly adapted to a transitory stage of new normal. Warren Buffet has a terrific saying, "It's only when the tide goes out that you can see who's swimming naked!" How can you use observations and learnings from a low-tide environment to create long-term development plans? When movement into a new normal highlights previously unrecognized development needs of your team members or the organization, capture it for what it is - an opportunity to grow.

The next phase of normal is unfolding today. Writing the next chapter in your organization's story means unceasing re-definition of normal, enabling leaders continually on the lookout for cues and clues to guide next steps, an essential element in *Leading from Zero*.

Chapter 4
Adaptive Disruption

In the early 1990s, management thought leader Peter Drucker shared a stage with then Ford Motor Company CEO, Red Poling. Poling gave an impassioned talk about Ford's new approach to vehicle quality. Through lean production and Deming-style statistical quality control, Poling believed Ford could achieve a level of product quality *as good as* Toyota's.

Following World War II, Japanese manufacturers in general, and Toyota in particular, focused on developing reliable, high quality, reasonably priced products. American producers focused on vehicle style and comfort while overlooking quality as a differentiator. By the 1980's, Toyota became a market disruptor in the U.S., aggressively taking share from domestic rivals by offering better quality, lower-priced cars.

After many references to his goal of building cars that were as good quality as Toyota, Drucker interrupted the CEO. In his deep, deliberate Austrian voice, he said, "Mr. Poling, the premise of your focus appears to me to be wrong. It seems to me you are forgetting that you are CEO of *THE* Ford Motor Company – the company Toyota and most other automobile manufacturers in the world have tried to emulate for much of this century. Why would you now want to emulate what

Toyota has done in following your company? Isn't the question you should be asking, 'What do automobile buyers want and how do we provide it?'"

For a moment, this Fortune 100 CEO was speechless. He processed Drucker's question, prepared to respond, then paused again. Finally, he said, "Professor Drucker, we honestly haven't thought about it like that." Poling paused again, then closed with, "I will go back to my team and pose that question to see where it leads us."

The moral of this story is that when a business or industry experiences *asymmetrical threats* – new competitors, alternative operating models, divergent paradigms - there is a tendency to study the disruptors and ask, *How can we be more like them?* The *adaptive disruption* principle says to effectively interpret asymmetrical threats as clues that customers' needs, interests, and values may be changing. Rather than study what disruptors do, we go to the source – our customers – to deepen our understanding of what matters to them. To borrow from Drucker's line of inquiry with Red Poling, the real questions are: *What do our customers want? Are their needs something we can effectively address?* and *How do our organizational competencies lend themselves to addressing recognized and unrecognized needs?*

Asymmetrical disruptors are prevalent in retail, manufacturing, distribution, supply chain management and many technology verticals. Consider the current state of the financial services industry. Financial technology companies or *fintechs* dominate headlines by deploying new ways of addressing old problems like opening accounts, making payments and modeling investment portfolios. Bank CEOs pulled into the wake-turbulence of these disruptors make statements like "we are really a technology company" or "we're becoming more agile in our development process like a start-up." Nice concepts, yet emanating from the wrong question – *how can we be more like the disruptors* – not *what do our customers want and how can we deliver it?* Putting the proverbial cart before the horse.

Leaders are called to look beyond current conditions, while not overlooking today's reality. That means asking *what's next?* The Red Poling story is rich with adaptive disruption lessons that help define what's next:

- *Start with your customer* – Gather candid input to deeply understand what customers expect today, what they anticipate they'll need tomorrow, the value they place on what they want (aka: their willingness to pay for it) and why they'd leave your offering for an alternative. Do not rationalize what you hear. Look for recognized needs as well as those that may not yet be recognized. Use these learnings to create a picture of the future state experience your organization will deliver. This picture can then be distilled into a roadmap to create your future state customer experience.

- *Know what it takes to earn and re-earn your relevance* – With clarity about customer expectations, take a fresh view of your business. Imagine you are on the outside looking in at the needs to be addressed (the way external disruptors see your business). If you were completely unattached to legacy approaches for serving customers' needs, how would you navigate the business? How would you deliver what your customers need in the way they expect to experience it? This exercise can be a challenge due to the tendency to limit creativity by saying, "That idea won't work because _____."

Don't prematurely box your firm into a paradigm that a disruptor will bulldoze. Call in professional help to work through ideation with your team when necessary. Remember – relevance is experienced in the moment, through the eyes of the beholder (your stakeholders). You can build goodwill with employees, customers, and other stakeholders, but its shelf-life is short, and must continually be re-earned through understanding and addressing needs.

- *Understand your organization's competencies* – You have competitive advantages and opportunities to build upon them. Identify them, articulate them, and use them as the foundation to grow from before looking to the next new thing. From the place of competencies, working from the inside out, you will garner the most from adaptive disruption exploration. Conversely, looking for disruption windows solely from the outside in can camouflage strengths available for fortifying your competitive position.

- *Own Change Leadership* – Leaders define a vision and engage people to deliver it. A clear vision of your business's future state must include how and where you deploy new tech and tools; the corollary is, absent a clear vision, tech deployments become fragmented and fail to meet expectations. With a clear picture of where your organization is going in the evolution of who you serve and how you deliver to customers, you are positioned to drive stakeholder engagement. Without broad engagement in creating your business's future state, change efforts are doomed.

This principle informs action as early clues of asymmetrical threats surface. An alternative to waiting to see how things play out, adaptive disruption requires well-thought-out tactics to evolve in parallel with changes in the organization's world.

Adaptive Disruptive Conversations

Leading from Zero assumes barriers to entry in an industry are perishable or are easily overcome, potential for new competitors is high, competitive advantages are temporary and pricing pressure is constant. Within this context, the Adaptive Disruption strategy takes ownership of activities within the organization's control and navigates those which are not to fulfil the vision. Stimulus is external; response is intentional and aligned with the organization's vision. Remaining aligned with the vision requires strategic conversation and contemplation to shape effective actions as disruption surfaces.

Conversation #1 – Revisiting Vision

Does the vision still fit our organization?

Vision is the future state and defines the organization's place in the world. It combines mission, purpose, and strategy. Vision connects what your organization does through its competencies to the external world.

As clues of emerging disruption and paradigm shift sprout up, revisiting the vision guides leaders through alignment assessment. While vision is enduring, it must be adaptive to assure the organization earns and sustains relevance. Adaptive Disruption strategy opens the door to refining vision, if necessary, to earn relevance.

A common organizational mistake is reacting to emerging paradigm shifts starting with financial decisions. Evidence of impending disruption causes a Pavlovian response to recast financial expectations, cut costs, or eliminate functions. These are not inherently poor actions, merely the wrong initial response to a changing environment. Numbers measure results, not why an organization exists. Starting with the vision enables a focus on cause, not effect.

Conversation #2

With disruptive indicators we're observing, what are the most important two or three strategic priorities to deliver beyond expected financial results over the next 36 months to enhance relevance with employees, customers, and stakeholders?

What prioritized activities should the organization engage in to fulfill its vision? With a clear future state picture, the organization prepares to translate its reaffirmed vision into refined priorities supporting an Adaptive Disruption strategy. Now the future state picture becomes actionable.

I read an article about the resurgence of something called Paint-by-Numbers.

The idea came about in the 1950's as a mix between a coloring book and painting on a canvass. By starting with a clear picture of the desired result (future state), then following a step-by-step framework, anyone can create something beautiful.

Bringing vision to life is similar; it is irrelevant unless it informs priorities, and those priorities define actions: painting-by-numbers.

Conversation #3

How well do our actions align with our company's vision?

Vision Drift is losing sight of the future state and, as a result, fragmenting attention, and distracting company resources. Close alignment creates better results. These questions help frame this conversation:

- Which of the activities we engage in are most closely aligned with our vision?
- Which of the activities we engage in are out of alignment with the vision?
- How are we assuring our team members engage in activities most closely aligned with our vision?
- As a leader, how effectively do I address activities taking place in the organization that don't appear to align with the vision?

Adaptive Disruption as an intentional strategy empowers leaders to earn and re-earn relevance with stakeholders while driving continual evolution of the organization toward manifesting the vision.

Launched in Hartford, Connecticut in 1906, the Fuller Brush Company built its brand on making home cleaning products sold by door-to-door salesmen. They trained the salesmen to be courteous, helpful, and resourceful in their sales calls. The company grew to annual sales of $15 million by 1925. By the end of WWII, sales were $25 million, then in 1960, the company generated $109 million in revenue; equivalent to $1 billion in today's dollars.

In the late 1950's, evidence of change grew. Fuller Brush men generally called on the lady of the house during the day to present the latest in-home cleaning products. As more women entered the workforce, fewer people were at home in the daytime when the Fuller Brush man came knocking at the door. Americans also became less tolerant of door-to-door salespeople calling unannounced.

Customers changed. Consumer expectations changed. The talent pool changed. In the decade from 1950 to 1960, the percentage of women in the U.S. workforce increased from 34% to 38%. Yet the Fuller Brush Company failed to adjust their customer engagement approach or recruit women salespeople. The company didn't look ahead to see what the future state might be. While cues of disruption presented themselves, the Fuller Brush Company missed their window of Adaptive Disruption. Therefore, it failed to re-earn its relevance. Customers, potential employees, and vendors looked elsewhere to fulfill their needs.

Participating in the Paradigm Shift

The notion that in normal times development of science is driven by compliance with what he called a *paradigm* intrigued Thomas Kuhn, a professor of the history and philosophy of science at the University of California, Berkeley. In Kuhn's words, a paradigm supplies puzzles for scientists to solve and provides tools for their solution. A crisis in science arises when scientists lose confidence in the ability of the prevailing paradigm to solve particularly worrying puzzles called *anomalies*. A scientific revolution follows a crisis when a new paradigm replaces the existing paradigm.

In *The Structure of Scientific Revolutions*, Professor Kuhn explained that a mature science experiences alternating phases of normal science and revolutions. In normal science, the theories, instruments, values, and assumptions which inform conventional wisdom remain static, permitting the cumulative generation of puzzle-solutions. During a scientific revolution, conventional wisdom gets redefined to permit the solution of the more serious anomalous puzzles that disturbed the preceding period of normal science.

Adaptive Disruption in business is analogous. Indicators of asymmetrical threats to the existing paradigm begin to emerge. Evidence grows across stakeholders – customers, employees, vendors – that a shift is unfolding. Deploying Adaptive Disruption requires leaders to play an intentional role in defining the next paradigm for their organization when early evidence of diminishing relevance of the prevailing conventional wisdom surfaces. This requires continuous monitoring and refinement to course-correct or redesign activities required to fulfill an organization's vision.

As Adaptive Disruption occurs, organization vision remains the focus; competencies guide the path to vision fulfillment. The relationship between an organization's competencies and vision is symbiotic. Competencies, the inherent strengths of an organization, are the things they do uncommonly well. They must inform vision, and the vision must align with these competencies. Building from strengths creates a foundation for an agile, adaptive organization *Leading from Zero.*

Chapter 5
Process Mindset

My dad had a friend named Ralph Berol in the business of manufacturing pens. His factory was in Los Angeles, where my family lived. At the time, Ralph's factory was not automated; all pen production was done by hand. When Ralph received large orders requiring quick fulfilment, he needed additional labor for pen assembly to meet customer expectations. To expand production capacity, Ralph asked friends to lend a hand and assemble pens in their homes. He paid one cent per completed pen. To earn extra money for our family, my dad always accepted Ralph's requests. Dad, mom, my brother, and I turned our kitchen table into a make-shift pen production operation.

My brother and I were in elementary school at the time and the opportunity to earn a penny for every pen we assembled was compelling. One hundred pens per kid meant earning more than our weekly allowance. Ralph delivered boxes containing pen components – an inner spring-loaded ink filler, a push-button click mechanism to engage the filler, the two-piece outer pen body and a silver or gold ornamental ring for installation between the top and bottom pen body pieces.

Our first pen assembly engagements were individual endeavors. Dad placed boxes of components on the kitchen table, we all took our seats, grabbed the pieces we needed, then assembled pens until fatigue set in or we completed the batch.

After completing our first few batches, mom introduced the idea of developing an assembly line process by breaking down pen construction into subassemblies. First step - install a filler into the bottom component of the pen body. Second, insert the push-button click mechanism into the upper body. Third, add the ornamental ring to the bottom pen body. Final step, screw the upper and lower pen body components together and place the completed pen into a box.

This process resulted in accelerating our family pen production work and increasing output capacity. Through this assembly line process, we hit our stride and produced 2,500 pens in a weekend.

Clearly defined processes enhance effectiveness, efficiency, and consistency across activities. The *Leading from Zero* Process Mindset anchors in three principles - activity-process connectivity is stronger when intentionally designed, every activity is part of a larger process, and every process must align with a purpose.

Activity-process Connectivity

Activities are building blocks for processes which support other processes across an organization. Process is a series of activities or steps taken to fulfill a purpose or achieve an objective. While precision functions – product assembly, manufacturing, surgery, piloting an airplane – require a well-documented, consistently repeatable series of steps, many business processes are not formalized. However, lack of formal documentation in no way negates existence of a process. These informal processes can be observed, defined, re-engineered, or discontinued.

Drawbacks to informal processes are inconsistency in performance of activities, overload of information required to properly perform activities, challenges identifying root cause of issues, and efficiency limitations. Imagine an emergency room team approaching an incoming patient in crisis without having a clear process for assessing the problem before beginning surgery. Scary, but that's exactly what happened at a hospital in San Francisco.

In *The Checklist Manifesto: How to Get Things Right*, Atul Gawande, a public health researcher and surgeon, described the scenario. The medical team began surgery on a man believed to have suffered a shallow stab wound. Unfortunately, after surgery began, surgeons noticed a much larger, foot-long wound, resulting from being impaled with a bayonet. The man's injury occurred at a Halloween costume party. The surgical team on duty failed to double-check with the patient to understand what kind of injury he experienced.

Dr. Gawande used this example and other case studies to espouse use of a simple process guide known as the checklist. In his words, "The volume and complexity of what we know has exceeded our individual ability to deliver its benefits correctly, safely, or reliably. Knowledge has both saved us and burdened us." Dr. Gawande's research points to improved safety, consistency, and efficiency resulting from use of simple, short checklists. "What is needed...isn't just people working together be nice to each other. It is discipline. We are by nature flawed and inconstant creatures. We are not built for discipline. We are built for novelty and excitement, not for careful attention to detail. Discipline is something we must work at.

Just ticking boxes is not the goal here. Embracing a culture of teamwork and discipline is."

A checklist is simply an aid – an easy-to-use method of documenting a process. Dr. Gawande's advice for using checklists applies to seeing activities as elements of a process:

- **Keep the Checklist Simple and Short:** When every detail of every step is laid out, it makes the checklist too bulky. It also turns into micromanagement. It is a guideline, not an instruction manual.
- **Use Different Types of Checks for Different Needs:** Critical tasks need different checks than complex tasks. Task checks, such as setting up regular testing for software code, should be applied to critical aspects of a project. These are the aspects that could easily slip a team member's mind but could make a big difference if forgotten about. For more complex areas of a project, it can be a good idea to set up communication checks. This means that if there's an area of a project that is expected to have potential setbacks, collaboration is key. It helps to remind people that while they are responsible for a task, they aren't working in isolation.
- **Checklists Can Be Used for Learning and for Reminding:** If there is an expert working on a project, their checklist should only be used to confirm they are completing each step. However, for someone with limited experience, a checklist can be used as a learning tool. This individual should read the checklist first, then use it to guide them through the process.
- **Test and Adjust:** It is rare to get a checklist perfect the first time around. Develop a checklist, put it into action, and observe its success. Evaluate which steps are

confusing or redundant. You can fix these as you work your way through the list.

Dr. Gawande's work has been applied in business and medicine with positive results. Researchers found that simply having the doctors and nurses in an intensive care unit create their own process checklists for what they thought should be done each day improved the consistency of care to the point that the average length of patient stay in intensive care dropped by half. Imagine what simple process definition can do in your organization!

Practicing the Process Mindset principle requires leaders to step back from any specific activity, understand its interconnectedness, its interoperability with other direct and indirect activities, then evaluate the most effective, efficient, consistently repeatable approach to performing the task in context of the broader organization ecosystem.

As applied to *Leading from Zero*, interoperability refers to the first element of the Process Mindset - the *activity-process* connectivity. Connectivity extends beyond a single process and emerges from the interaction of diverse activities. Leaders are accountable for identifying and understanding relationships and assuring continuous process improvement.

Smart manufacturing developments present *Process Mindset* learnings applicable to overall organization activity connectedness. In their study, *Interoperability in Smart Manufacturing: Research Challenges,*[13] researchers Abe Zeid, Sarvesh Sundaram, Mohsen Moghaddam, Sagar Kamarthi and

---

[13] https://www.mdpi.com/2075-1702/7/2/21/ht

Tucker Marion of the Department of Mechanical and Industrial Engineering, Northeastern University, explored the increasing need for interoperability at different levels of the manufacturing ecosystem in context of recent advances in manufacturing technology - cyber–physical systems, industrial internet, artificial intelligence, and machine learning.

In these researchers' words, smart manufacturing involves networking of heterogenous components and services that reside within the boundaries of a factory (e.g., integration of smart shop–floor devices) or beyond (e.g., integration of a manufacturing cell with a cloud-based service). The integration and networking of smart manufacturing components and services within and beyond the boundaries of the factory call for seamless exchange of information with syntax and semantics understandable by all the heterogeneous systems involved. This interconnectivity is interoperability - the ability of two or more entities (or processes) to interact and cooperate. The study's authors believe successful implementation of enterprise-wide interoperability would result in effective and smooth manufacturing operations, cost reductions, increased productivity, and product quality.

As applied to *Leading from Zero*, interoperability aligns with the first element of the Process Mindset - the *activity-process* connection.

Through the lens of the larger Process

Banking is a heavily regulated industry and satisfying regulatory requirements is non-negotiable. Yet, a common misperception - *policies and procedures are the same* - produces unnecessary inefficiencies in the way traditional banks serve customers. How does this happen? Banking regulations emanate from legislation or through creation by a regulatory agency, the Office of the Comptroller of the Currency for example. New regulations are disseminated to banks for interpretation through their compliance department. Bank compliance departments then distill each regulation into a policy to be followed by bank employees.

Most bank regulations impact consumers directly or indirectly, yet it is rare for a bank to define, design and deliver a customer-based process for policy (therefore, regulation) implementation. Banks often lose sight of the intent of a regulation, and by default apply the rule as a process itself. Paradoxical about this approach is that it's rare for a regulation to *define* a process. Banking regulators generally describe an expected outcome with a new regulation but leave process design to each bank. In this flexibility resides an opportunity for banks to design interoperable processes which satisfy regulators and address existing and emerging customer needs – earning and sustaining relevance.

Recognition that activities are part of some larger process, not standalone events, is a first step in evaluating consistency, effectiveness, and efficiency. The *Leading from Zero* premise – every organization starts its day from zero – requires intentionally defined, repeatable processes to assure earning relevance. Starting at zero, guided by the organization's vision, leaders must intentionally choose activities aligned with earning relevance across stakeholders.

Consider the example of commercial air travel. An overarching process encompasses a series of activities - subprocesses – to fulfill the purpose of transporting passengers and cargo safely. The flight itself is the larger process.

Supporting the flight are light and heavy aircraft maintenance processes, interior and exterior cleaning, preflight checklist procedure and fueling processes. Each individual procedure is part of a larger process. When each process is performed effectively, the outcome is more likely to fulfill the purpose. If a procedure is missed or performed ineffectively, fulfilling the purpose faces increased risk.

In 1982, Boeing introduced the 767, a twin engine, long-range wide-body airplane. The 767 could be configured to carry 269 passengers and cargo 6,500 nautical miles. The plane came equipped with three redundant hydraulic systems for operation of controls, landing gear, and utility systems and a Ram Air Turbine to power basic controls in the event of an emergency that compromised power. This feature saved the day in 1983 when an Air Canada 767 ran out of fuel during flight at an altitude of 41,000 feet.

Flight 143 originated in Montreal, with a scheduled stop in Ottawa in route to Edmonton. Pilots and ground support technicians performed their preflight procedures as required. One step involved accessing information provided by the Fuel Quantity Information System Processor (FQIS) which controls fuel pumps and feeds information to the plane's fuel gauges. Due to a sensor malfunction, the FQIS didn't work that day, leaving the 767 without operating fuel gauges. However, redundancies existed to navigate this type of event.

In this situation, plan 'B' called for the flight maintenance crew to calculate fuel in the 767's tanks manually by a process known as "dipping the tanks" - the jet plane version of using an oil dipstick in a car - to determine onboard fuel volume. Fuel technicians cautiously worked through their calculations to assure sufficient fuel for the scheduled flight.

Employee training is an important subprocess supporting the macro-process of completing safe flights. In this case, the flight maintenance crew had not been trained to perform manual fuel dip calculations. Since technicians were unfamiliar with this process on the new Boeing 767, they re-ran measurements three times for an accurate read. With proper training, they would have known the 767 used all metric measurements; instead, they assumed U.S. measurements in assessing fuel levels. One kilo equals 2.2 pounds, so their measurements overstated fuel on board by about double.

At the first stop in Ottawa, the 767's fuel tanks were re-dipped, and again, the measurements overstated fuel by double. Actual fuel onboard totaled 9,144 kilos at departure from Ottawa. Fuel required to reach Edmonton was about 20,000 kilos.

Over Red Lake, Ontario, a warning light came on in the cockpit informing pilots of a fuel pressure problem with the left engine. Soon, a second fuel pressure warning light illuminated. After evaluating the situation, the pilot prepared for an unscheduled landing in Winnipeg. As the plane descended to an altitude of 28,000 feet, the left engine flamed out. Moments later, starved of fuel, the right engine failed. Miscalculating fuel in the plane's tanks turned this new Boeing 767 into 132-ton glider.

The outcome of this experience could have been tragic, but a series of factors came together to prevent disaster. When both engines failed, the 767's Ram Air Turbine deployed, descended from the plane's undercarriage and activated the wind-driven fan supplying hydraulic pressure necessary to operate certain fight controls. This back-up system bought pilots time to develop a plan to land their aircraft.

In addition to commercial aviation experience, the plane's pilot, captain Robert Pearson, had experience as a glider pilot, a skillset that elevated his ability to navigate this extraordinary situation. However, Winnipeg airport was beyond glide range, and no large airports existed in the area, limiting landing options. Co-pilot Maurice Quintal introduced an alternative to a commercial airport. While in the Royal Canadian Air Force, Quintal had been stationed at a now abandoned base in Gimli. He knew the site's runways were long enough to land the 767 and suspected the base lay within glide range. Quintal and Pearson performed glide speed and descent calculations with support from air traffic control to pinpoint their landing at the Gimli base.

As the Gimli runways came into line of sight, Pearson noticed a large group of people congregated at the site. The runways had been turned into an auto racetrack. That Saturday afternoon they hosted the Winnipeg Sports Car Club's Family Day event. When people at the track saw the big plane coming in, they scattered as fast as possible to get out of the way.

Through deft aviation skill, captain Pearson overcame lack of drive brakes and engine controls to slow the plane to landing speed. The second the rear wheels hit the ground the captain pumped the brakes. Two tires blew out. The front landing gear had not properly locked into place and collapsed as the front wheels hit the runway, causing the plane's nose to skid on the tarmac. Miraculously, there were no injuries from the landing.[14]

This story provides a dramatic illustration of the *Process Mindset*. Training is an important, ongoing process in an organization, not a standalone event. This training process is aligned with a purpose – assuring that all employees are fully

---

[14] http://hawaii.hawaii.edu/math/Courses/Math100/Chapter1/Extra/CanFlt143.htm

enabled to accurately, competently, perform their jobs. The training subprocess supports the larger process of safely transporting passengers and cargo.

Less dramatic, yet aligned with the *Process Mindset* principle, are activities like new product development, manufacturing, marketing, business development, distribution, and the customer experience, all of which contribute to earning, re-earning, and sustaining relevance as an organization.

Process aligned with Purpose

Process needs purpose. It goes without saying. Or does it? A recent study by OnePoll[15] found that one-third of office-based employees' time is wasted on *pointless* business processes. Fifty-one percent of the survey's 5,000 respondents said outdated business processes were preventing them from doing their jobs properly. The need to assure process relevance, alignment with purpose, extends beyond office workers.

Robotic Process Automation (RPA) is technology that emulates human activities within digital systems to create and automate rules-based business processes. RPA enables process streamlining, efficiency and reduced operating costs. In their *Harvard Business Review* article *Before Automating Your Company's Processes, Find Ways to Improve Them,*[16] authors Thomas H. Davenport and David Brain wrote, "In many companies, the level of process knowledge and understanding is quite low. The company may have collections of standard

---

[15] https://www.financialdirector.co.uk/2019/06/19/how-inefficient-processes-waste-nearly-a-third-of-employees-time/
[16] https://hbr.org/2018/06/before-automating-your-companys-processes-find-ways-to-improve-them

operating procedures, but they are often poorly documented and out of date. Each employee typically follows their understanding of best practices."

Davenport and Brian are proponents of RPA: "What sets RPA apart from other automation technologies is that its ability to imitate a human user of one or more information systems reduces development time and extends the range of functions that can be automated across a much wider range of business activities." They qualify their views, writing, "To be clear, however, the match between RPA and business processes isn't a perfect one if the goal is to redesign or improve the process rather than to automate its current state, quoting the words of process management expert Andrew Spanyi[17], who said, 'RPA does not redesign anything. It doesn't ask whether we need to do this activity at all. It operates at the task level and not the end-to-end process level.'"

This underscores the importance of defining process purpose in context of earning relevance. Absent clear purpose underlying a process, resources are distracted, misallocated or inefficient, even with use of cutting-edge software like RPA. Establishing the processes purpose results from answering three questions:

- Is this process necessary in executing our business strategy; if so, why?
- What is the expected outcome of the series of activities which comprise this process?
- If we didn't perform this process, how would we achieve the expected outcome?

---

[17] http://www.spanyi.com

Process Mindset Applied

Leaders demonstrating the Process Mindset discern interconnectedness of activities, see activities as part of a larger process aligned with a purpose. By intentionally framing activities in a process context, leaders reduce risks resulting from individual differences in selecting activities to perform, decrease the likelihood of employees overlooking necessary steps for successful task completion, and create a structure for continuous improvement.

Strategy development is deductive, beginning with defining a future state vision. The picture of what things will look like because of intentional business activities is deconstructed into strategies, implemented through activities. Process definition is inductive, aligning activities which support strategy implementation, in a sequence that optimizes efficiency and effectiveness. Process design provides a connecting point between vision and execution to assure activities produce desired outcomes. By integrating top-down with bottom-up approaches, leaders create an environment biased toward activities designed for purpose fulfilment.

Putting the Process Mindset into practice requires five steps:

- Affirm a clear future state vision for your organization.
- Assess each strategy for alignment with the vision.
- Assess each activity supporting a strategy for alignment.
- Evaluate activities for interconnectedness with others' process connectivity.
- Bundle connected activities into processes, designing for efficiency and effectiveness.

Each step requires studied, purposeful diagnostics, candid evaluation, and openness to redesign. The payoff for operating with a disciplined Process Mindset is a more closely aligned organization, positioned to earn and re-earn relevance with its stakeholders every day.

Chapter 6
Seeing Your Organization as Others Do

"Mirror mirror on the wall, who's the fairest of them all?" Grimm's fairy tale tells the story of an evil queen in a distant land. Each time she asked this question of her magic mirror, she heard the same answer: "Thou, O Queen, art the fairest of all." This pleased the queen since she knew her magical mirror spoke nothing but the truth.

One fine morning the queen asked, "Mirror, mirror on the wall, who's the fairest of them all?"

The mirror's answer shocked her. "You, my queen, are fair; it is true. But Snow White is even fairer than you."

The queen reacted with rage. "Huntsman, take Snow White into the woods and kill her. When you come back be sure to bring Snow White's heart as proof she is dead."

The huntsman took Snow White into the forest but found himself unable to kill her. Instead, he let her go and brought the queen the heart of a wild boar as evidence he completed his assignment.

Seeing ourselves as others see us challenges our nature. While self-awareness is unique to the human species, we are generally poor judges of the way others perceive us. Social science research tells us we often overestimate our level of self-awareness. We feel we know and understand ourselves, and how others see us, better than we do. To try to see ourselves objectively can trigger difficult-to-process feelings. Consequently, we avoid, minimize, or rationalize observations we don't like. Our brains are wired for fight or flight, which predisposes us to protect ourselves against negative feedback.

Like the evil queen, our bias is to see ourselves in a favorable light. We emphasize our positives, discount our negatives. Organizational research supports this. Studies show employees routinely rate themselves above average relative to their peers. A classic study, *Participation and the Appraisal System,* by John French, Jr., Emanuel Kay, and Herbert H. Meyer, researched performance self-assessments at a General Electric plant in 1965.[18]

This study analyzed 92 performance reviews. On average, reviews covered 32 specific performance items with positive appraisals on 19 items and negative on 13. Praise more often related to general performance characteristics, while criticism usually focused on specific performance improvement items.

When receiving feedback, the average employee reacted defensively to seven of their manager's critiques during the appraisal meeting (about 54% of the time). Observers recorded denial of shortcomings cited by the manager, blaming others, and excuses as defensive reactions.

Managers rarely observed constructive responses to critiques. The more negative feedback the employee received during the performance appraisal meeting, the more defensively he reacted (all participants were men in this study).

---

[18] https://hbr.org/1965/01/split-roles-in-performance-appraisal

Researchers posit one explanation for defensiveness: the difference between an employee's self-assessment and the manager's appraisal.

The most interesting take-away from this study: On average, employees perceived their performance to be *above* average in their self-assessment. Only two of the 92 participants estimated their performance below average. For the remaining 90 employees, the average self-estimate of performance was at the 77th percentile, which means the average employee saw themselves as 27 points above average, a *statistically impossible result!* The evil queen's reaction in the story of Snow White was extreme. Feeling shocked by uncomfortable feedback is common.

Seeing ourselves objectively as individuals is a challenge. Is the dilemma different for our organizations?

Yes and no.

Organizations are complex social networks comprised of individuals, therefore subject to human conditions. Seeing our organization as others do is critical to earning, re-earning, and sustaining relevance.

How do organizations overcome the natural tendency toward not being objective?

Globally, companies spend $50 billion annually on market research to understand customers, market trends, competition, and how the market perceives a business and its products. An abundance of available feedback provides leaders rich insights into how others see their organization.

Direct, unvarnished views on how employees and customers see a business, accessible through Glassdoor, Foursquare, Yelp, Angie's List, Slant, and others, enables leaders to put themselves in the shoes of their most valuable stakeholders.

Stakeholder insights and research become valuable when they inform actions that lead to better employee and customer experiences, greater value-add, or identification of blind spots in the way a company shows up.

Yet, even with the petabytes of data companies gather about their customers, preferences, behaviors, and perceptions about relevance are overlooked. Why?

Organizational Self-Awareness

Organizational self-awareness means understanding stakeholders' perceptions of how the company shows up. Leadership literature is flush with material on the importance of individual self-awareness. Ingredients for leadership success include the ability to monitor ourselves, attune to our emotions and understand how we come across to others, read our audience, and make adjustments to meet situation-specific needs.

Effective self-awareness shines a light on blind spots, informs actions, sets parameters for reactions, and empowers a feedback loop that reflects the impact of our words and actions. People who demonstrate heightened self-awareness are more effective leaders. Absent self-awareness, people in leadership positions appear tone-deaf, out of touch, ignorant or arrogant. Organizational self-awareness is a corollary. The company fuels this *Leading from Zero* strategy when it institutionalizes mechanisms to override natural blind spots, including employee and customer feedback assimilation processes, peer listening reviews, issue recognition forgiveness, find it/fix-it empowerment, and new employee observation downloads. These five activities help acquire and sustain a clear view into the way your company is perceived.

Implement employee and customer feedback assimilation processes. The purpose of each feedback process is to gather stakeholder observations while overriding the tendency toward Situational Attribution - attributing the cause of perceptions (behaviors) to a situation or event outside a person's control rather than an internal characteristic.

Practice a well-defined, ongoing method for acquiring and assimilating perceptions reflective of the organization's relevance to its stakeholders is core to *Leading from Zero* recognition that relevance is re-earned daily. Assimilating employee and customer perspectives are essential ingredients to relevance. Leaders must recognize they own the organization's vision; stakeholder perspectives on relevance informs them how effectively stakeholders interpret steps to implement the business vision. An effective process for assimilating perceptions from employees or customers about your organization includes:

Obtain feedback from employees and customers through multiple comfortable, safe channels. A single-channel approach (i.e., employee engagement surveys) will miss opportunities with stakeholders uncomfortable in the chosen format. For example, customer focus groups can generate candid feedback. However, participants differ in comfort levels with direct, forthright, in-person sharing. Conversely, online surveys invite anonymous feedback to specific questions. At the same time, this platform allows biases (i.e., answering survey questions the way respondents believe they are expected to answer), and exaggerated feedback (amplifying a complaint or compliment). Using multiple channels to gather diverse input yields actionable feedback.

Engage objective, candid feedback trustees, advisors who act in the organization's best interest when they share unvarnished feedback to inform actions. Advisors can be consultants, customer user groups, advisory board members, community influencers, or other external observers willing to share feedback in the company's best interest.

Commit to receive feedback without judgement. To withhold root cause analysis of a perception until feedback is sufficiently received is difficult and requires discipline to fight urges to defend, rationalize or explain the situation while gathering feedback. For the company to commit to suspend analysis, judgement, blame, or reaction requires practice, but pays a valuable dividend in the form of deep awareness of the organization's relevance with stakeholders.

Peer Listening Reviews

Each manager in an organization lives a unique experience of its activities that informs individual perspectives. These views can be mined to stretch organizational self-awareness.

Peer-to-peer listening can be simple – recurring one-to-one meetings between two managers with an agenda covering observations of the organization overall and areas of responsibility for each manager in the meeting. The approach can also be formal, documented and disseminated across the management team.

I led the integration of two investment businesses combined as part of a bank merger. The firm my company acquired experienced two years of investment client attrition. Bank advisors self-reported the best information available about why clients left, which raised questions about report validity. I needed to understand how past clients perceived the firm and why they left.

I called dozens of departed clients and heard stories describing a common set of reasons they chose not to do business with our firm. While painful to hear feedback, I didn't like, I gained powerful information directly from clients about why they decided to leave.

I wanted managers to also experience hearing directly from clients. I believed they would benefit from learning that we could address issues we learned about with minor adjustments in our client engagement approach. I also recognized these managers had a natural tendency to defend their own client perceptions and see employees who reported different perceptions to them in an unfavorable light.

Instead of managers reaching out to departed clients from their own regions, we established a process for calling those served by other regions. Weekly, each manager received a list of recently departed clients from one of seven regions other than their own.

We developed a simple questionnaire – what did we do wrong, what could we have done different, what should we have known about your expectations of us that we didn't, what would it take to re-earn your business. Instead of reporting feedback to me, I asked each manager to share what he or she learned from departed client phone calls with their peer in the region that served the client.

The objective was to create a safe environment for peer listening and learning. Results far exceeded my expectations. Managers learned from their peers how their advisors and the firm were perceived by former clients. They used this input to refine client engagement activities, document client expectations and formalize a manager-client communication protocol.

Issue Recognition Hold-harmless

"The first messenger that gave notice of Lucullus' coming was so far from pleasing to Tigranes that he had his head cut off for his pains; and no man dared to bring further information. Without any intelligence at all, Tigranes sat while war was already blazing around him, giving ear only to those who flattered him."

Greek philosopher and author Plutarch made it clear in *Lives of the Noble Greeks and Romans* that the bearer of bad news faces existential risks. Conversely, penalizing the messenger does not further organizational self-awareness.

According to Gallup,[19] when things go horribly wrong for a business, two factors are almost always true: Someone in the company knew about the issue and someone didn't speak up. More than likely, they didn't speak up because they couldn't be bothered, or they feared retaliation. Unfortunately, many leaders attempt to patch over these systemic problems with policy changes when the underlying issue is cultural.

To embed a hold-harmless commitment into organizational culture enables team members to explore opportunities and see things as do other stakeholders. By removing fear for potential bearers of any news – good, bad, or neutral - the organization multiplies its points of observation and insight. Confident

---

[19] https://www.gallup.com/workplace/323165/why-isn-brand-bigger-data-point-one-answer.aspx

employees rise to expectations for issue recognition, articulation, and resolution.

Earning and sustaining relevance requires continually refreshing an organization's understanding of its stakeholders' perceptions. Leaders own accountability for sustaining a fearless culture which welcomes issue identification and resolution and recognizes bad news doesn't get better with time.

Find It/Fix It Empowerment

Empowering employees to find and fix issues that interfere with the customer experience is a corollary to the Hold-harmless principle.

Gallup says, "A [company] culture that doesn't handle problems well is especially damaging when those problems are connected to customers. Gallup has discovered that customer relationships can be saved *and strengthened* when customers feel heard, businesses genuinely apologize, and something is done to make things right. How to 'make things right' will depend on that customer's unique needs. How that customer feels about the way their issue was handled will significantly affect their opinion of your business and their recommendations to others."

Empowered employees are themselves stakeholders in your organization. Enabled with ability to make things right for customers, they inform perspectives (customers' and other stakeholders) and demonstrate the organization's authentic commitment to earning and sustaining relevance daily.

New Employee Observation Downloads

When my family moved from a single-story home to a split-level, we saw and heard things from a new perspective. The home, situated in a quiet neighborhood, featured upstairs bedrooms. My bedroom had an outdoor deck, and we often slept with the slider door open at night. The first couple of weeks living in that home, I heard birds chattering late into the night and early in the morning. I loved their sounds – they created a calm, tropic feel in our suburban neighborhood.

After a month, I no longer noticed the birds singing when I went to bed. I didn't hear them in the morning. The birds were still there, and when I focused my listening, I heard them. But our new home now felt and sounded normal. Things that caught my attention in the beginning no longer stood out.

New employees to your organization have an experience like mine settling into a new home. When they first arrive at your company, they will see and hear things that capture their attention. Once they acclimate, these stand-out observations will lose their attention-grabbing newness, then fade into business-as-usual patterns.

Capturing the power of first impressions is a valuable practice in organizational self-awareness. Initial observations, documented and shared, provide a meaningful source of insight so you can see your organization as others do.

When I interview or hire a new team member, I invite first impression feedback. I want to know what my business does that doesn't make sense, seems out of date, out of touch, or lands flat on a stakeholder. I know the window of objectivity closes quickly and want to capture insights as early in the relationship as possible.

Leaders focused on building and sustaining organizational self-awareness seek honest feedback from fans and critics, demonstrate authentic curiosity about how their company is perceived by stakeholders, and earn relevance by adjusting activities that interfere with the way others see them.

Insular Organizations

Building organizational self-awareness acumen and seeing our organization as others do requires intent, open-mindedness, and discipline. Absent this discipline, an organization can become insular.

Insular organizations rationalize divergent perspectives about their appearance. They denigrate feedback and attribute dissonant input to misunderstanding the company's countenance.

Acceptant leaders do not defend or rationalize stakeholders' perceptions. They recognize stakeholders are the beneficiaries of their work and essential to the company's economic viability and success.

I held a management assignment with a bank that took great pride in its culture. The company used a rigorous hiring process comprised of eight to ten interviews for management positions to assure potential employees aligned with the culture.

The company believed when many people interviewed a candidate, they would weed out culturally misaligned applicants. Only those demonstrating a strong cultural fit would progress through the bank's elaborate candidate screening.

The bank also held high expectations for attracting, hiring, retaining, and promoting candidates representing a rich array of diversity dimensions and backgrounds. Executives were assigned clear, compensation-linked objectives to increase diversity of employees with new hires.

I was often a candidate's final interviewer. I interviewed people for management jobs within my business line, and for other parts of the company. After a half-dozen interviews, I noticed a pattern. Candidates came in different shapes, sizes, cultures, and orientations, but everyone I interviewed sounded alike. They didn't use the same words or deliver responses to my questions in a similar way; the root lay deeper. They *thought* alike.

By the time a candidate came to me for an interview, they had already been through at least seven prior sessions. I learned the only candidates who made it to that point in the process had already been identified as demonstrating a good cultural fit. Well-qualified candidates holding different perspectives were unlikely to advance in the process. Homogeneity of thinking unintentionally emerged as a cultural characteristic. The bank's interviewing process only allowed hiring people who thought and sounded like those already part of the company.

The bank's intentions were reasonable – assure new hires fit the culture. Their process contributed to creating an insular organization – one with a narrow range of sources for new ideas, unique perspectives, or challenging voices. While the company believed it attracted diverse new talent, instead it reinforced established mindsets and fortified insular views with each new employee.

When I recognized this pattern, I changed my approach as an interviewer. In place of standard questions, I opened with,

"Now that you've been interviewed by so many leaders in this company, tell me two or three things we do here that don't make any sense."

I followed with, "If you were CEO of this company, what are the top five things you would do different than today?"

I wanted to see the company the way outside, independent thinkers saw us. If a candidate couldn't step beyond our existing insular thinking, I didn't support advancing them in the interview process.

Leading from Zero holds transparency is a fundamental characteristic, recognizes relevance is in the eye of the beholder, and that beholders see everything. The process of earning and sustaining relevance requires leaders to actively seek, acknowledge, accept, and address candid feedback about how the organization is seen by its stakeholders – employees, customers, and partners.

The role of stakeholder observations

Organizational vision is the litmus test for assimilating perspectives about how your organization is perceived by others. It provides context in answering the question: What do we do with stakeholder perspectives we gather? What observations can we distil into actions to move the organization toward its vision and contribute to earning relevance with stakeholders?

Observations that push a company away from its vision dilute relevance.

There is a difference between understanding how a company is perceived by its stakeholders and innovation.

Steve Jobs said, "It's really hard to design products by focus groups. A lot of times, people don't know what they want until you show it to them."

Creating new products speaks to addressing realized and unrealized needs. Consumers didn't know they needed an iPhone, but when a product satisfied the need for information, entertainment and communication, users recognized a way to make their lives simpler, which created demand.

The relationship between an organization and its stakeholders is dynamic – always in motion. *Leading from Zero* positions the organization to lead the relationship by staying attuned to observations, becoming aware of unintentional missteps in the relationship, and adjusting course in alignment with vision when evidence says relevance is at risk.

Chapter 7
Winning Hearts and Minds: The Human Element of Leading from Zero

He that complies against his will
Is of his own opinion still
Which he may adhere to, yet disown,
For reasons to himself best known

From *Hudibras* by Samuel Butler

I met Paul while in the management training program at Bank of America. Paul, Regional Vice President in charge of commercial banking activities across the territory I worked in, oversaw a hundred employees and millions of dollars in revenue to the company. Paul occupied a big corner office in the building where he spent much of his time in meetings with clients, management, and community leaders. He was usually the first person at work in the morning and the last one to leave at night.

Paul's assistant managed his calendar. One morning I went to her desk to schedule an appointment for Paul to meet a prospective new client with whom I worked. As she paged through his calendar to find a time, I saw that appointments filled almost every minute of every day. Most days Paul participated in client breakfasts, lunches, dinners and plenty of appointments and meetings in between. Yet, despite a very full schedule, Paul always found a way to engage with his team. He asked employees about things they were working on, if there were any challenges standing in their way, and how he could help them make their day a success.

As a trainee, I considered myself one of Paul's lowest priorities, but he didn't see it that way. He made a point of stopping by my desk at least weekly to say hello, get to know me, and learn about my experience as a trainee. After a couple of months on the job, Paul's assistant came to my desk and said "Paul would like to take you to lunch tomorrow. Are you available?" Of course, I said yes.

At lunch, Paul focused on me and expressed genuine interest in how I thought I could make an impact on the company. He said, "Tell me about one of the clients you're working with and how your work helps them, our team, and the Bank of America."

That compelling question, placed me in a position to think through my contribution to the stakeholders I served – clients, my teammates, and the company. I hadn't thought about my role in those terms prior to that conversation. Since that day, I've repeated the question – What is my role in serving the stakeholders that matter most?

One-to-one and across the entire team, Paul won hearts and minds. He created emotional engagement to a vision that included performing meaningful work for a noble purpose. Paul understood the importance of earning and sustaining relevance with his stakeholders and embraced the process. He embodied the human element of *Leading from Zero*.

Creating Esprit de Corps

The practice of earning and sustaining relevance with stakeholders every day can only happen through synchronizing people, priorities, processes, and technology with activities designed to manifest an organization's vision. People set priorities they believe will achieve the vision, distill priorities into activities, align activities into processes, then implement technology in support of process execution.

Avia Pervia – Latin, meaning *make the difficult things simple* is a wonderful adage for the way we do business. Companies often over-index technology as *the* solution to make things simple and eliminate problems. Invest in the right platform or tools, and difficult processes become simple. Companies spend billions every year to create greater efficiency, build better products and do so more cost-effectively, yet the return on technology investment often falls short of expectations. In most cases, shortcomings are not due to priorities, process design, or technology.

So, what's left?

Investing in the human side of organizational progress can be an afterthought with some companies. Consider the Boston Consulting Group's findings: only 17% of companies that neglected culture during digital transformation efforts were able to improve performance, 90% of companies focusing on digital *culture* reported breakthrough or strong financial performance. Almost 80% of companies that focused on culture were able to sustain strong or breakthrough performance.

BCG's *It's Not a Digital Transformation Without a Digital Culture*[20] report says, "Being a digital organization means not only having digital products, services, and customer interactions, but also powering core operations with technology. Becoming one, therefore, requires a tectonic change in the *activities* employees perform as well as in their individual behaviors and the ways they interact with others inside and outside the organization. Although it should come as no surprise that the traditional ways of working are incompatible with the new ways, it often does."

This principle applies beyond digital transformation endeavors. Bain & Company studied the question: Why is it so difficult to make change take root? In *Results Delivery: Busting Three Common Myths of Change Management,*[21] the firm reported their study of barriers to successful change management at 184 global companies. They found 65% of initiatives required "significant behavioral change on the part of employees — something managers often fail to consider and plan for in advance." In addition, 63% of companies analyzed faced "high risks to their change efforts because of significant communications gaps between the leaders of the effort and the employees most affected by it." Bain found many companies assume they can succeed with the right combination of strong incentives for their leaders, yet they overlook the importance of building employee commitment during a change effort.

In *Beyond Performance: How Great Organizations Build Ultimate Competitive Advantage,* authors Scott Keller and Collin Price speak to the genius of *and* – focusing the organization on

---

[20] https://www.bcg.com/publications/2018/not-digital-transformation-without-digital-culture
[21] https://www.bain.com/insights/results-delivery-busting-3-common-change-management-myths/

performance *and* health. Keller and Price work from a traditional definition of *performance:* What an enterprise delivers to its stakeholders in financial and operational terms, evaluated through measures including net operating profit, return on capital, total return to shareholders, net operating costs and stock turn. They describe three key attributes of good organizational health: Internal alignment, quality of execution, and capacity for renewal. Keller and Price developed a definition of *Organizational Health* consisting of nine elements:

- **Direction** – a clear sense of where the organization is heading and how it will get there that is meaningful to all employees.
- **Leadership** – the extent to which leaders inspire actions by others.
- **Culture and climate** – the shared beliefs and quality of interactions within and across organizational units.
- **Accountability** – the extent to which individuals understand what is expected of them, have sufficient authority to carry it out, and take responsibility for delivering results.
- **Coordination and control** – the ability to evaluate organizational performance and risk, and to address issues and opportunities when they arise.
- **Capabilities** – the presence of the institutional skills and talent required to execute strategy and create competitive advantage.
- **Motivation** – the presence of enthusiasm that drives employees to use extraordinary effort to deliver results.
- **External orientation** – the quality of engagement with customers, suppliers, partners, and other external stakeholders to drive value.

- **Innovation and learning** – the quality and flow of new ideas and the organization's ability to adapt and shape itself as needed.

Organizational Health is something leaders can control and holds a causal relationship with results. Through Keller and Price's research and anecdotal observation in their work at McKinsey & Company, they believe at least 50 percent of an organization's long-term success is driven by its health.

University of Florida professor Philip Podsakoff's research spans the fields of management, marketing, psychology, and organizational behavior, with a focus on leadership effectiveness and consequences of Organizational Citizenship Behaviors (OCBs). OCBs are often referred to as "helping" behaviors – things like altruism, courtesy, cheerleading, peacekeeping, sportsmanship, civic virtue, and conscientiousness.

Dr. Podsakoff's research in this area includes a study with Scott MacKenzie titled *Impact of Organizational Citizenship Behavior on Organizational Performance: A Review and Suggestion for Future Research*. This research suggests OCBs may contribute to organizational success by (a) enhancing coworker and managerial productivity, (b) freeing up resources so they can be used for more productive purposes, (c) reducing the need to devote scarce resources to purely maintenance functions, (d) helping to coordinate the activities both within and across work groups, (e) strengthening the organization's ability to attract and retain the best employees, (f) increasing the stability of the organization's performance, and (g) enabling the organization to more effectively adapt to environmental changes.

Podsakoff suggested that OCBs may help enhance an organization's ability to adapt to changing environments in several ways. For example, when employees who are in close contact with the marketplace volunteer information about changes in the environment and make suggestions about how to respond to them, it helps an organization adapt. Similarly, when employees voluntarily attend and actively participate in meetings (civic virtue), it may enhance an organization's responsiveness by aiding the dissemination of valuable information. In addition, when employees exhibit sportsmanship by demonstrating a willingness to take on new responsibilities or learn new skills, it may enhance an organization's ability to adapt to changes in its environment.

Adages like *greasing the skids* and *one hand washes the other* get at the spirit of helping behavior in an organization. People like helping people who help them. Developing and sustaining a helping culture pays significant dividends. Wharton psychology professor Adam Grant summarized Podsakoff's research[22] writing, "helping-behavior facilitates organizational effectiveness by:

- Enabling employees to solve problems and get work done faster
- Enhancing team cohesion and coordination
- Ensuring that expertise is transferred from experienced to new employees
- Reducing variability in performance when some members are overloaded or distracted

---

[22] https://www.mckinsey.com/business-functions/organization/our-insights/givers-take-all-the-hidden-dimension-of-corporate-culture

- Establishing an environment in which customers and suppliers feel their needs are the organization's top priority."

Each of these studies are connected by a thread which addresses an essential theme: to earn and re-earn relevance, an organization must win the hearts and minds of its employees by creating a pull toward the vision. Vision and values have a symbiotic relationship; each informs the other, and both must distill into attitudes, relationships and activities aligned with manifesting the vision. Steve Jobs said, "If you are working on something exciting that you really care about, you don't have to be pushed. The vision will pull you." To this I add if a leader doesn't win the hearts and minds of team members, there is little chance of the organization earning and sustaining stakeholder relevance.

Creating esprit de corps – group spirit - is an essential, intentional leadership activity. Leaders must create and sustain an environment where people are empowered to make an impact through their ideas and actions, aligned with the organization's vision. Connection to the vision contributes to group cohesion. It creates emotional engagement to the purpose of work performed. Fostering this emotional engagement begins with understanding the team members' experience – what the organization represents through what it does in the eyes of the employee. In a word, empathy.

Before John Mayer and Peter Salovey coined the term *Emotional Intelligence*, Ronald Riggio, professor of Leadership and Organizational Psychology at the Claremont McKenna

College Kravis Leadership Institute introduced the Social Skills Inventory (SSI). SSI assesses six basic social skills that underlie social competence. It evaluates verbal (social) and non-verbal (emotional) communication skills and identifies strengths and weaknesses. Dr. Riggio's research using the SSI covers management and leadership as well as other social applications. His framework categorizes basic social skills into three types - skills in encoding (*expressive* skills), decoding (*sensitivity* skills), and ability to regulate or control communication. These three basic skills operate in the nonverbal domain (dominated by skill in emotional communication), and the social domain (dealing primarily with the verbal/social aspects of communication skill).

Riggio's work included studying the connection between social skills and empathy, and as an undergraduate student, I had the opportunity to work with him on this research. *Social Skills and Empathy,* by Ronald E. Riggio, Joan Tucker, and David Coffaro, suggested that on the surface, empathy appears governed by sensitivity skills, however, other basic social skills must be implicated for successful empathic communication. For example, an individual who is emotionally empathic needs to be sensitive to another's emotional state but must also be able to reflect the emotion back to the individual, indicating they vicariously feel the same emotion. Therefore, successful emotional empathy would be a combination of the basic skills of emotional sensitivity and emotional expressivity.

Similarly, cognitive empathy, dominated by the skill of social sensitivity (i.e., ability to decode and interpret verbal communication and an understanding of social norms), also involves the basic social skills of social expressivity and social control. To successfully take another's perspective and communicate a cognitive understanding of the individual's position, the empathic person must be a skilled verbal communicator and a controlled and polished social actor (role playing ability is central to the basic social skill of social control).

Professor Riggio's conclusion: Empathy is a combination of basic social skills which individuals can draw upon. For leaders this means consciously practicing their skills in encoding, decoding, and ability to control their communication. A key take-away is the notion that empathy is a combination of skills – skills that can be *developed, practiced,* and *improved* over time. Riggio's Social Skills Model and the SSI have been used for assessing and developing basic communication skills essential for effective leadership. Riggio and other researchers have identified many ways in which emotional skills contribute to effective leadership, ranging from the expressive skills required to motivate and inspire followers to emotional sensitivity to develop close interpersonal relationships and to the ability to control and regulate emotions in order to effectively play the role of leader. Mindfully practicing the social skill set known as empathy plays a meaningful role for leaders in winning the hearts and minds of their team members.

Creating emotional engagement with the business's vision, practicing empathy, managing organizational health, and sustaining a culture that fosters helping behaviors contribute to esprit de corps.

Engaging Co-ownership

When I became head of Investment Management & Trust at Wells Fargo in 2003, the business needed a strategy overhaul. I joined the company two years earlier to work with the business unit head as chief operating officer to help change a trajectory of declining client retention and shrinking revenue. The manager who hired me focused on a short list of *his* priorities for the business. His team made progress on his priority list, but results we not moving in the right direction.

When my manager moved on to another position, the company asked me to take his place leading the business. My new boss said: "This business can be whatever you want it to become. I'll support you with the resources you need. Your job is to develop the strategy and 'sell it' to your team." His message created a contrast with my predecessor's approach of developing a list of priorities to "fix" the business, absent input from anyone on the team.

I had observations and analysis about what the new strategy should include from my time as chief operating officer. As much as I wanted to start sharing my ideas about the business's future, I forced myself to take a different approach. In my first 90 days in my new position, I met with managers, individual contributors, peers, and partners across the company to hear their ideas on opportunities, issues, priorities, and concerns. Every week, I visited a different location, accompanied by members of my direct report team so we could compare notes about what we learned.

After the first month of these idea gathering meetings, clear patterns informing what the strategy should be emerged. Some of the themes aligned with what I perceived before spending time with so many team members, but others were beyond my prior ideas. By the time I had visited every major market in which the business operated, the new strategy had practically written itself.

I saw as the most remarkable part of my learning tour the level of engagement people exhibited about contributing to our emerging strategy. Many team members told me they had never been asked for their input on what the business should do to better serve clients and grow. I used my airplane time flying home from meetings to summarize my notes, then share them with meeting participants. After emailing notes to each group as follow-up, I invariably received Thank You notes expressing excitement about where things could go in the business.

Creating a new strategic plan became a simple process of distilling, reframing, and documenting priorities and activities people who worked in the business every day had defined. The overarching lesson I learned was about the power of co-ownership. I didn't need to have all the answers. What I did have to do was ask the best questions I could of my team and other stakeholders, then listen closely to hear what mattered most. That didn't mean I wouldn't contribute my own ideas or challenge assumptions and suggestions. It meant I had to create an environment of strategy co-ownership with the people who would determine the level of success we could achieve.

Engaging co-ownership in defining, designing, and delivering the Investment Management & Trust strategy in the early 2000s worked. Throughout the decade, the business grew through a co-owned four pillar plan – strong client retention, developing new client relationships, effective risk management and economic stewardship. Management reinforced co-ownership of the operating plan monthly through activity reviews and performance deconstruction and with an annual plan refresh meeting. Leaders across the business held conversations with their team members in advance of the annual meeting to hear their ideas on opportunities, issues, priorities, and concerns with the business. Each leader in the business contributed their team's input to the annual meeting for distillation into an updated plan for the new year.

Co-ownership refers to shared dominion over creation of an organization's future state. Future state is defined through the vision which informs an organization's activities. This shared dominion must be built into the organization's culture. Here are five conversation topics to discuss with your team members to evaluate their level of co-ownership of your business vision and activities:

- Which elements of the organization's vision resonate most and least with you and why?
- How does the vision align with the target customers the business serves?
- How does the work you do each day directly connect with fulfilling the vision?
- What is the degree of alignment working toward a common purpose between departments in the organization?
- Where do you see gaps in the level of accountability for activities that bring the vision to life?

A few years ago, I contributed 360-degree feedback about a colleague who had begun working with an executive coach. The new coach facilitated conversations with people who worked closely enough with this executive to have meaningful observations about the way he showed up in his work. The coach asked me, as part of gathering my feedback, how I thought my colleague's employees perceived him.

She asked, "How would his employees rate him on the 'hot coal' test."

I wasn't familiar with that reference, so I asked, "Could you elaborate?"

She said, "Would his team members be willing to walk barefooted across hot coals if he asked them to do so?"

This dramatic metaphor determined how effectively my colleague connected with his people.

Fortunately, its rarely necessary to ask people to travers hot coals in business these days. However, leaders often make extraordinary requests of team members who only rise to the occasion if they feel an emotional engagement to the organization. Winning hearts and minds of team members is an ongoing endeavor that must come from a place of authenticity from leaders. Consistency in demonstrating actions covered in this chapter builds necessary trust with team members.

Chapter 8
Sustainability

One night, after a baseball game, three umpires decided to go out for pizza and talk about the games they each worked that evening. They entered the restaurant, ordered their pizza, then sat down and began conversing. Conversation quickly moved to one of the most difficult challenges umpires face - calling balls versus strikes. The first umpire confidently affirmed, "There are balls and there are strikes, and I call them as they *are!*" The second umpire, with a furrowed brow said, "That's not true. There's balls and strikes, and I call them as I *see* them." Finally, the third ump said, "You're both wrong. There's balls and there's strikes, and they ain't nothin' till *I call 'em.*" In business, like baseball, much of perceiving, defining, interpreting, and acting is in the eyes of the beholder.

A macroeconomic extension of the umpire story is provided by University of Chicago professor Robert Lucas. Dr. Lucas received the 1995 Nobel Prize in Economics for his development of Rational Expectations theory. He determined that individuals make personal economic decisions based on past experiences and anticipated results. In other words, aggregate collective expectations determine macroeconomic outcomes.

This inductive view suggests individual economic perceptions and expectations affect behavior; aggregate behavior defines the condition of the overall economy. When we expect favorable economic conditions, we act accordingly, spending money, circulating the flow of resources, which results in a stronger economy. Conversely, when we feel concerned about the economic future, we are more likely to hold on to money, spend less, and behave in a manner consistent with economic contraction. Paraphrasing the words of the third umpire, *the economy ain't nothin till we call it something*.

Since future expectations influence economic decisions made by individuals today, it is easy to see similar behavioral patterns in organizations. Expectations inform business performance, even during uncertain operating environments. When employees expect the unexpected, they tend to adapt better to dynamic circumstances. When we expect business success through satisfied customers, behavior tends to follow, assuring satisfied customers.

Research tells us that emotionally intelligent employees are more likely able to *predict* environmental uncertainty, adapt to environmental changes, solve problems, and show creative performance in dealing with colleagues and customers.[23]

A step between understanding or even predicting a dynamic operating environment and evolving to thrive under developing conditions is new learning. *Leading from Zero* holds organizational learning as an ongoing process, not episodic.

---

[23] *Emotional intelligence and creative performance: Looking through the lens of environmental uncertainty and cultural intelligence*, Mahlagha Darvishmotevali, Levent Altinay, Glauco De Vita, *International Journal of Hospitality Management* Volume 73, July 2018, Pages 44-54
https://www.sciencedirect.com/science/article/abs/pii/S0278431917301081

Learning organizations fuel sustainability of *Leading from Zero* principles.

Management, Science and Technology researchers Marjolein C. J. Caniels and Simone M. J. Baaten at Open University of the Netherlands published a study titled *How a Learning-Oriented Organizational Climate is Linked to Different Proactive Behaviors: The Role of Employee Resilience.*[24] Caniels and Baaten identified a relationship between a learning-oriented organizational climate, employee resilience and proactive behaviors. Their research posits employees who perceive a learning-oriented organizational climate will demonstrate a high level of resilience. In organizations demonstrating a learning-oriented climate, employees are likely to feel free to take the initiative to experiment, take risks, and propose creative ideas.

Over time, this positive attitude towards experimentation and accompanying misses and errors builds resilience. Employees experiment more, take charge more often, express their voices and innovate frequently, as they do not fear repercussions for failure. Employee resilience and the capability to adapt in the face of taxing circumstances promotes proactive behaviors, including improving work methods, influencing colleagues, and championing ideas to others. Resilience actively stimulates employees to take control of and bring about change within the organization.

Strategic Resilience

On September 11, 2001, the United States entered uncharted territory. Some compared the attack on New York's Twin

---

[24] https://link.springer.com/article/10.1007/s11205-018-1996-y

Towers to Pearl Harbor sixty years earlier. Those who only knew of Pearl Harbor through their study of history saw no comparison. The event caused a tremendous direct and indirect human toll. No playbook existed for how to feel or react. Americans were shocked, shaken, and uncertain. That uncertainty manifested in the business world as well. Capital markets tumbled and shockwaves reverberated through the entire economy.

The company I worked for at the time didn't have any employees directly impacted by the attack, but the first message from our CEO focused on making sure all team members and their families were safe. His next communication following the attacks focused on proactively engaging with our clients. As a bank, he knew when our team members experienced uncertainty, our clients were likely to be concerned about their financial well-being, and our responsibility was to express empathy and support.

The CEO then delivered a remarkable message. Widespread confusion raged as capital markets and businesses reopened and searched for a new footing. In mid-September, many companies were developing business plans and budgets for 2002. How could you plan for the next calendar year when you didn't know what the next week would reveal?

My company had just completed our first round 2002 plan and budget the first week of September. The process involved each line of business leader, like me, submitting our first draft annual plan to the Chief Financial Officer and CEO. They aggregated all line of business plans from across the company, interpreted the big picture plan, then if necessary, went back to line of business leaders to request any adjustments necessary to meet overall company goals.

First draft plans were submitted Friday, September 7th.

The CEO's email to business line leaders said, "I've never been through anything like this before. This business environment is unexpected and what comes next is uncertain. What I am confident about is why we're here. Our vision is to help our customers experience success in their financial lives. That is not changing. As we work together though this uncomfortable time, let's stay focused on why we're here. To accomplish our vision, let's also look for opportunities to recruit more top talent from other firms that may not be as clear. This is the time for us to bring in more top performing talent, new customers and grow our company."

Some companies allowed uncertainty, discomfort, and fear to put everything they did on pause. They took the path of waiting to see what happened next to decide what they should do in their business.

This CEO took a different perspective. He anchored his team in the company's vision. He didn't overlook extraordinary conditions redefining business activities; he locked on to the horizon while navigating waves of uncertainty. He demonstrated *Strategic Resilience*.

President Franklin Roosevelt is credited with saying, "A smooth sea never made a skilled sailor." As optimistic as this sentiment is, it doesn't diminish the fact that sailors can experience acute queasiness when circumnavigating billowing whitecaps. Strategic Resilience compels leaders to interpret rough waters as invitation to experience new levels of success.

Strategic Resilience is the practice of thinking forward while leading through turbulence and adapting to difficult operating circumstances while looking beyond current conditions to keep focused on the horizon. In the context of *Leading from Zero*,

Strategic Resilience is a strategy for embracing dynamic fluidity in the operating environment.

Holding this dynamic perspective helps leaders synchronize their organizations with the reality of fluidity. Practicing Strategic Resilience requires accepting asymmetrical change as the norm. Team members look to the organization's vision and values instead of specific practices, products, operating goals, or legacy accomplishments as touchstones.

A recent Gallup study cites *resilience* as a make-or-break trait for organizations during tough times like 9/11 or the COVID-19 pandemic. Gallup found, "Thriving and resilient cultures endure through good times and bad. These cultures prove their endurance during tough times by experiencing minimized disruption of key outcomes, such as productivity, customer service and profit. Resilient cultures *survive*. Even during good economic times, new threats to organizations are constant -- and constantly changing. *Thriving, resilient cultures see accelerated performance compared with their peers.*[25]

Here are five practices to raise strategic resilience acumen as a leader:

- **Acknowledge current reality** – When times are uncertain, the operating environment is rapidly changing, and status quo is anything but status quo, call it what it is – fluid, dynamic and uncomfortable. Finding the right balance between acknowledgement and

---

[25] From Gallup, *Is Your Culture Resilient Enough to Survive Coronavirus?* by Jim Harter, May 20, 2020 https://www.gallup.com/workplace/311270/culture-resilient-enough-survive-coronavirus.aspx?utm_source=workplace-newsletter&utm_medium=email&utm_campaign=WorkplaceNewsletter_Jun_06092020&utm_content=5keyelements-cta-1&elqTrackId=78aa69c6485347c9bfd858a055ced845&elq=e642439ed5df44a298b8689b1a8b6884&elqaid=4245&elqat=1&elqCampaignId=901

wallowing can be a challenge. Still, leaders own the tone and are accountable for moving the organization through describing the condition into action; positioning the condition is simply context.

- **Re-connect with your vision and values** – The world outside your organization changes quickly. You adjust operating activities accordingly. But your business vision is focused on the horizon and remains more constant. Vision is the future state picture an organization strives to create and results from *what* we do, *why* we do it, and *how* we fulfill our mission. Values are core beliefs which define what the organization stands for. Values stand even more static than vision. In the words of *Good to Great* author Jim Collins, "Every institution has to wrestle with a vexing question: What should change and what should never change? Timeless core values should never change; operating practices and cultural norms should never stop changing." Reconnecting with your organization's vision and values provides comfort in a storm and true north through all conditions.

- **Communicate touchpoints for stability, including a focus on the future** – Leaders are called to look beyond current conditions. That doesn't mean having a crystal ball. It does mean sustaining dialog around the question - *What's next for our organization*? With vision and values as points of stability, articulating the view toward the horizon draws attention forward, beyond current uncertainty. Engaging team members in the long game contributes to an organization's strategic resilience.

- **Define what success looks like today, in this moment; adjust as the future unfolds** – Goals are generally established on a quarterly or annual basis. When operating conditions change rapidly, goals must be redefined in context of current, dynamic reality. Team members perform at their best when they know what success looks like and when expectations are aligned with dynamics of the environment. Per Gallup, "During tough times, employees need managers who reset priorities, involve them in reestablishing their goals and constantly clarify their role relative to their coworkers."

- **Swim with the current** – A rip current is a powerful, narrow, fast-moving channel of water that starts near the shore, with a strong pull toward breaking waves. According to the National Oceanic and Atmospheric Association, if you experience rip currents when swimming at the beach, the best way to avoid drowning is to stay calm, avoid fighting the water's movement and swim parallel to the shore. Fighting the current exhausts the swimmer, jeopardizing the likelihood of a safe return to shore. Said another way, fighting the current is not a path to success. For leaders, this translates to *understanding* rip current-like changes in the business environment's flow, quickly *adapting* to condition changes, and keeping sight of the vision and *opportunities* for accelerating progress (aka, returning to shore).

Strategic Resilience as a practice enables leaders to renew esprit de corps, focus their organization's activities and make strategy work.

Change Leadership

Human beings are wired for free will. Change requires us to alter established, comfortable, behavior patterns. Self-imposed change, redesigning our patterns based on our internal desire for different outcomes, is challenging. There can be an additional layer of resistance in an organizational setting, where change is triggered by someone or something outside ourselves, because the motivation stimulating behavioral pattern redefinition is not our own.

The term "reactance" refers to a feeling that our behavioral freedoms or choices are being taken away. As leaders, we must attune to the emotional side of change that takes place within the people being asked to refine their activities.

Change leadership draws on inspiring participation in the transformation at hand, motivating behavior, inviting co-ownership of tactics, and sustaining focus. Recognizing the human dimensions of change, here are five actions to increase effectiveness as a change leader:

- **Vision**. Successful change efforts begin with a clear picture of the organization's future state and why fulfilling the vision matters. Vision clarity, with a succinct rationale for the direction forward, provides a foundation for the inspiration necessary to overcome inertia and resistance to change. Creating buy-in to the vision is a first step toward opening minds to the introduction of the new behavioral patterns necessary to make and sustain change.
- **Engagement**. Stakeholders need to feel emotionally engaged in where the organization is going, the steps in the journey and their role in fulfilling the vision. Provide a compelling picture of what your

organization wants to demonstrate to create the touchstone for emotional engagement and give the change endeavor traction. Engagement is the vehicle through which leaders invite team members to co-own the change effort and all tactics of implementation. As a result, team members feel motivated.

- **Overcommunication**. Regular communication with stakeholders on the organization;s goals, including progress and accomplishments toward the change vision, creates transparency. Regular communication is not enough. Team members need an extraordinary level of information, in small, digestible servings, to stay connected to the change story. A well-defined messaging framework for the change effort, including why a shift is necessary, how implementation is progressing and what the future state will look like are pillars for communications tactics.

- **Actualization**. Success in a change effort is usually experienced through a series of outcomes which bring specific results to life. Drawing attention to the actualization of deliverables, which aggregate to become the future state, offers team members a sense of accomplishment. The gestation cycle for meaningful change efforts tends to be measured in quarters or years, so presenting evidence of progress frequently is essential to sustaining focus.

- **Reinforcement**. Muhammad Ali said, "It's the repetition of affirmations that leads to belief. And once that belief becomes a deep conviction, things begin to happen." Reinforcement takes place through frequent reaffirmation of the future state vision, the roadmap, and the progress being made toward bringing the vision to life.

Every leader has a decision to make -- initiate change or react to pressures forcing the organization's evolution. Effective leaders proactively look for opportunity to preemptively refine processes, increase efficiency and improve products and services to their customers. Intentionally designing a compelling future state vision that wins hearts and minds of team members is core to making change management work.

Sustainability in Practice

Leader expectations influence activities within an organization. When leaders recognize the dynamic flow of their operating environment and sustain expectations around perpetual adaptation to evolving conditions, employees are empowered to define, design, and deliver *Leading from Zero* strategies. Within this context, sustainability means continually earning organizational relevance when conditions for relevance are subject to ongoing evolution - different today than yesterday or tomorrow. Sustainability is experienced through:

- **Regularly refreshing organizational expectations in alignment with the operating environment.** As the external environment evolves through new customer needs, expectations, and alternatives, business expectations are redefined within context of the organization's vision.

- **Functioning as a learning organization, grounded in the lifecycle of knowledge and skills.** New strategies develop to propel the business on the path to earning relevance with stakeholders, requiring ongoing knowledge acquisition and upskilling of employees. Concurrent with changing knowledge and skill requirements is the progression of job descriptions. This process is deductive, starting with the picture of what the organization expects to contribute to its stakeholders. Ingredients included in each job description contribute to defining how the vision is fulfilled. The learning organization continually develops individual and collective knowledge and skills to re-earn stakeholder relevance.

- **Individual and organizational resilience** – In his 1966 hit song *That's Life*, Frank Sinatra sang, "I've been up and down and over and out and I know one thing. Each time I find myself flat on my face I pick myself up and get back in the race." Individual resilience is the ability to return to "the race" of life in the face of adversities. Resilience enables people to recover from setbacks and overcome challenges by finding a new path toward their goals. In a leadership context, resilience includes guiding the organization forward while leading through difficult operating circumstances; recognizing challenges in current conditions while focusing on what can be accomplished toward the vision.

- **Intentionally demonstrating and buoying positive urgency in matters of pressing importance**. In *A Sense of Urgency*, Harvard Business School professor emeritus

John Kotter explains that, "Urgent behavior is not driven by a belief that all is well or that everything is a mess but, instead, that the world contains great opportunities and great hazards." Kotter also wrote, "Urgent action is not created by feelings of contentment, anxiety, frustration, or anger, but by gut-level determination to *move, and win, now*. These feelings quite naturally lead to behavior in which people are alert and proactive, in which they constantly scan the environment around them, both inside and outside their organizations, looking for information relevant to success and survival." As a self-initiated process, urgency contains an element of enthusiasm in terms of focusing authentic energy into exploring an idea or action designed to earn and re-earn stakeholder relevance.

- **Change leadership** – Adapting to change is reactive; initiating change is proactive. Change leadership is grounded in proactive identification of opportunities to achieve gains in stakeholder relevance.

Each element of sustainability is a process. Expecting the unexpected, anticipating uncertainty and aligning with changing conditions are characteristics of *Leading from Zero*. Sustaining these processes requires recognition that the business environment is dynamic, in perpetual motion. When leaders embrace these sustainability perspectives, team members learn *they* are change agents with their fingers on the pulse of dynamic operating conditions outside and within the organization. Leaders set the tone by defining their organization as living, breathing, learning ecosystems, reflecting aggregate motion and sentiment of their members.

Sustaining relevance with stakeholders requires ongoing observation, awareness, understanding and adjustment to the dynamic environment.

Chapter 9
Leading from Zero in Practice

In a recent Wall Street Journal interview, General Motors CEO Mary Barra was asked about electric vehicle manufacturer, Tesla.[26] Wall Street Journal's Mike Colias asked, "Tesla's market valuation is now roughly 10 times that of GM's. How do you and your team talk about that internally?"

Ms. Barra's response could be straight out of the *Leading from Zero* playbook. "You don't have a *right* to win. You have to *earn* the right." (italics added).

Colias continued, "What can you do so that GM gets more credit for your electric vehicle strategy?"

Barra's response, "I think that will come when we put more proof points out there...*We* have to remember that General Motors sells more vehicles in this country than anyone else. *We* have a relationship with the customer. How do we build on that success and *clearly demonstrate* we're going to be in a leadership position in the future?"

Barra recognized relevance must be earned. Through its actions, her company will sustain meaningfulness, pertinence, and value or become irrelevant. *Leading from Zero* is a strategic leadership paradigm executed through seven essential elements for earning relevance.

Conditions define this paradigm to which all organizations are subject. These conditions – *the dynamic nature* of the operating environment, *resource development* as a differentiator, ongoing expectations for *greater value* and consistently demonstrating *efficiency gains* – inform leaders' decisions.

Relevance is earned and sustained through Seven Essential Elements:

- Leading by Cause

---

[26] The Wall Street Journal, 9/4/2020, *Up Against Tesla, a Pandemic and Lagging Share Price, Mary Barra Steers GM Forward*

- Unceasing Re-definition of Normal
- Adaptive Disruption
- Process Mindset
- Seeing Your Organization as Others Do
- Winning Hearts and Minds
- Sustainability

Failure to earn and sustain relevance leads to a cycle of organizational demise.

Leading from Zero Paradigm Conditions

- **Operating Environment Dynamic** - The business landscape is a dynamic environment, in perpetual motion. Aligning expectations to continuous motion empowers adaptation to changing conditions.
- **Resource Development as a Differentiator** – Competition for valuable resources is intense. This condition necessitates conscious decisions about an organization's resource management philosophy - consumption or development. Resource development leads to differentiation.
- **Self-Initiated Disruption** – With perpetual motion as the nature of business, disruption is an expected condition. Leaders make an intentional decision to proactively engage through self-initiated disruption or react to the condition. Through preemption, leaders uncover choice; reaction offers few options.
- **Continually Adding Greater Value** – Stakeholders always expect more benefit and value from the organization. Embedding this understanding in the

business aligns expectations of all contributors to the company's endeavors.

- **Consistently Demonstrating Efficiency Gains** – Identification of better ways of operating is the modus operandi for the benefit of employees, customers, and owners.

Practicing the Seven Elements of Earning Relevance

Leading by Cause

Key Ideas:

- We manage cause; we can only measure effect.
- Focusing only on results can lead to inaccurate conclusions about business performance.
- Cause-based analysis of results seeks to understand the behavioral factors contributing to outcomes.
- Understanding root cause avoids under-estimating or over-simplifying what it takes to create better outcomes.

Actions:

- Deconstruct results thoroughly to determine *the* root cause of results.
- Use financial results as a reverse roadmap through understanding why a strategy works or falls short of producing expected outcomes.
- Engage in cause-based conversations when reviewing results with team members. What were sales activities last month that created these results? What changed in our business development

activities last quarter vs. the same period last year? Which customers did we focus on? How did we engage those customers? How did they react to what we have to offer? What is getting in the way of our new business development activities? What has changed in the competitive environment?

- Focus attention on mindful selection of operating activities today as ingredients creating desired results tomorrow.

Unceasing Re-definition of Normal

Key Ideas:

- What we perceive as *normal* is simply a point on a continuum of dynamic change to which we become accustomed.
- The next phase of normal is a continually evolving story for the organization to write.
- The question for leaders is: What comes next?
- As the operating environment changes, sustaining a focus on what your company does (mission), why you do it (purpose), and how you fulfill your mission (strategy) leads to greater organizational stability.

Actions:

- Create a rolling quarterly strategic plan to enable adaptability, in context of the long-term view, as the operating environment changes.
- Revisit the organization's vision frequently to assure it remains relevant as conditions change.
- Identify areas for intentional discontinuation of activities, processes, products, or services which no

longer serve the business. This can free-up capacity to apply more impactfully in the next new normal.

- Seek opportunities for new offerings that address customers' evolving needs as conditions change.
- Capture development opportunities with team members and the business model which surface as the organization seeks adaptation to a new normal.
- Swiftly identify and address points of resistance to change (Legacy Fallacy, Denial of Imminent Change Indicators, Unconventional Wisdom, Fear of Change, Bureaucratic Inertia, Comfortable Critical Mass Mindset).

Adaptive Disruption

Key Ideas:

An alternative to waiting to see how things play out, Adaptive Disruption requires well thought out tactics to evolve in parallel with changes affecting the organization's world.

- As early clues of asymmetrical threats - new competitors, alternative operating models, divergent paradigms – surface, leaders identify activities within the organization's control, navigate those which are not to fulfil the vision.
- Revisiting the organization's vision in context of external changes enables leaders to adjust priorities, activities, and strategy, adapting to disruption.
- Risk of Vision Drift - fragmenting attention, and distracting company resources – is magnified when external threats increase.

- Reacting to emerging paradigm shifts with financial decisions before thoroughly diagnosing conditions, is an ineffective response to a changing environment.

Actions

- Address asymmetrical threats, draw from customers insights and expectations.
- Play an intentional role in defining the next paradigm for your organization when early evidence suggests diminishing relevance of the prevailing model.
- Understand changes to what your customers want as conditions change.
- Determine whether your business can effectively address emerging customer expectations, and how your organizational competencies lend themselves to addressing recognized and unrecognized needs.
- Imagine you are on the outside looking in at customer needs to be addressed (the way external disruptors see your business) and analyze where vulnerabilities or gaps exist in your business model.
- Identify and articulate your organization's competitive advantages and opportunities to build upon to optimize adaptive disruption exploration.
- Own change leadership by championing a vision of where your organization is going in the evolution of who you serve and how you deliver to your customers.

Process Mindset

Key Ideas:

- Every activity is part of a larger process.
- Every process must align with a purpose.
- Activity-process connectivity is stronger when intentionally designed.
- Intentional process design provides a connecting point between vision and execution to assure activities produce desired outcomes.
- Process definition is inductive, aligning activities which support strategy implementation in sequence to optimize efficiency and effectiveness.

Actions

- Bundle connected activities into processes designed for efficiency and effectiveness.
- Evaluate specific activities in context of interconnectedness with other direct and indirect activities, then evaluate the most effective, efficient, consistently repeatable approach to perform the task relative to the broader organization ecosystem.
- Identify and understanding relationships between activities aggregated into processes as a step toward continuous process improvement.
- Define process purpose by asking: Is this process necessary to execute our vision and business strategy, and if so, why? What is the expected outcome of the series of activities involved in this process? If we didn't perform this process, how would we achieve the expected outcome?

- Regularly assess activities for alignment with strategies they support and interconnectedness with other processes.

Seeing Your Organization as Others Do

Key Ideas:

- Organizational Self-Awareness is understanding stakeholders' perceptions of how your company shows up.
- Leaders own the organization's vision; stakeholder perspectives on relevance inform how effectively they interpret activities to implement the vision.
- Leaders focused on building and sustaining organizational self-awareness seek honest feedback from fans and critics, demonstrate authentic curiosity about how their company is perceived by stakeholders, and sustain relevance by adjusting activities which interfere with the way others see them.
- The relationship between an organization and its stakeholders is always in motion, requiring leaders to stay attuned to their perceptions, observations, and reactions to unintentional missteps by the business, adjusting course in alignment with vision when evidence says relevance is at risk.
- Capturing the power of first impressions from new employees, customers and stakeholders is a valuable source of insight to how your organization is perceived.

Actions:

- Institutionalize mechanisms to override natural blind spots, including employee and customer feedback assimilation processes, peer listening reviews, issue recognition forgiveness, find it/fix-it empowerment and new employee observation downloads.
- Distill observations into actions that move the organization toward its vision and contribute to earning relevance with stakeholders. Recognize observations that push a company away from its vision and dilute relevance.
- Commit to receive feedback without judgement, blame, or retribution to the messenger.
- Engage objective, candid feedback trustees – advisors, consultants, customer user groups, advisory board members, community influencers, or other external observers - willing to share feedback in the company's best interest.
- Draw upon multiple channels to gather diverse observer input to yield actionable feedback.

Winning Hearts and Minds

Key Ideas:

- To earn and sustain relevance, an organization must win team members' hearts and minds by creating a pull toward the vision.
- Leaders have a duty to curate an environment where people are empowered to make an impact through

their ideas and actions, aligned with the organization's vision.

- Creating emotional engagement with the business's vision, practicing empathy, managing organizational health, and sustaining a culture that fosters helping behaviors contribute to esprit de corps.
- Co-ownership refers to shared dominion over creation of an organization's future state, defined through the vision which informs an organization's activities.

Actions:

- Actively engage in defining, designing, and delivering a culture where team members co-own the organization's path forward.
- Recognize as a leader you set the tone for active engagement in nurturing esprit de corps.
- Articulate how your organization's vision aligns with target customers the business serves; speak to the connection between team members' daily activities, serving customers, and fulfilling the vision.
- Assure activity and objective alignment between departments to avoid team member disengagement due to working cross-purpose.
- Identify and address accountability gaps in performing activities that bring the vision to life.

Sustainability

Key Ideas:

- Sustainability begins with expecting the unexpected, anticipating uncertainty and aligning with changing conditions.
- Leaders are called to look beyond current conditions, sustaining dialog on the question: What's next for our organization?
- Leaders have a decision to make: initiate change or react to pressures forcing the organization's evolution.
- Implementing new strategies to propel the business on the path to sustaining relevance requires ongoing knowledge acquisition and upskilling of employees. Organizational learning as an ongoing process fuels sustainability of *Leading from Zero* principles.
- Strategic Resilience is thinking forward while leading through present turbulence; adapting to difficult operating circumstances while looking beyond current conditions to focus on the horizon.
- With asymmetrical change as the norm, the organization's vision and values become touchstones for stability.
- Sustaining relevance with stakeholders requires ongoing observation, awareness, understanding and adjustment to the dynamic environment.

Actions:

- Acknowledge current reality in the operating environment, with balance between recognizing favorable and uncomfortable conditions as context, and the direction forward as empowerment.

- Re-connect the organization with its vision and values to draw focus to the horizon.
- Define what success looks like today, adjust as the future unfolds. People perform at their best when they know what success looks like and when expectations align with environmental dynamics.
- Function as a learning organization, grounded in the lifecycle of knowledge and skills to sustain stakeholder relevance.
- Lead through resistance to change, building buy-in to the vision, creating emotional engagement with the direction forward, overcommunication about what the future state looks like, highlighting actualization of activities moving the business forward and reinforcement of core messages.
- Demonstrate and buoy positive urgency in matters of pressing importance. Self-initiated urgency with enthusiasm focuses authentic energy into exploring an idea or action designed to sustain stakeholder relevance.
- Embrace *Leading from Zero* sustainability activities to empower team members as change agents; they are closest to dynamic operating conditions outside and within the organization.

Chapter 10
Strategic Leadership

The Seven Essential Elements of *Leading from Zero* provide a strategic path to earning and sustaining relevance with stakeholders. Navigating this path is Strategic Leadership – seeing the big picture and important details at once, assimilated to inform activities today, tomorrow, and beyond. This discipline manifests through continually evolving the organization's paradigm while operating effectively in the current environment – managing strategy as an ongoing process. Strategic Leadership is about achieving balance between today's reality and tomorrow's aspirations by applying the Seven Essential Elements of *Leading from Zero*.

Leaders taking the long view benefit from engaging team members in creating co-ownership of the future-state vision. Earning and sustaining relevance with stakeholders requires alignment between long-term vision and current activities, while practicing versatility in the path taken. Versatility may feel antithetical to a strategic plan. After all, aren't strategic plans immutable blueprints?

When I taught a college course in strategic management, the notion of strategy as a fluid process, not a static document, created confusion with some of my students. How can an organization be clear in its path forward and malleable as conditions change? Strategic Leadership creates balance across today, tomorrow, and beyond; business vision serves as a fulcrum for balance. Future state vision describes a destination; the path – strategy – changes as conditions shift. When environmental changes accelerate, holding the future in sight with details of today's reality in mind becomes essential.

Zooming In and Out

My grandmother was a world traveler, an adventurous spirit who loved exploring new places, people, and cultures. When she returned from a trip, she invited my family to her home to share a destination slide show and share the story of her journey. Hearing Olga's stories from Asia, Egypt, Europe, Africa, and South America was mesmerizing.

Grandma Olga's travels stretched my understanding of the world. As a young boy, the world was defined by my home, neighborhood, and school. It was hard to assimilate more of the world than the city of Downey, California.

During a conversation about her visit to Egypt, I asked grandma how big the world was. Olga opened a National Geographic magazine with an image of the Milky Way galaxy. She held a magnifying glass to a tiny speck in a swirl of blue and white lights on the page, pointed with a sharp pencil and said, "This is our world. When you look at the big picture, the world is small." Her point: context matters. The world is large from a child's perspective. From the universal view, it's small.

Strategic Leadership requires contextualization - understanding, interpreting, and distilling large swaths of data and determining how they inform actions aligned with the organization's vision, today, tomorrow, and beyond.

Wharton Professor Jerry Wind and his colleagues Colin Crook and Robert Gunther discussed this challenge in *The Power of Impossible Thinking*. They wrote, "Given that we make sense generally of only a small portion of the available external sensory stimuli to construct a coherent picture, we face several challenges in sifting through an avalanche of information. The first is to make sure we pay attention to the relevant portion so our perspective is not built upon shifting sands or the wrong information. We do this by zooming in and examining interesting details closely. This helps us identify dis-confirming information that should cause us to challenge our broader models. The second challenge is to make sure we can gain sufficient perspective to create a coherent picture at all. We do this by zooming out and looking at the big picture."

Strategic leaders cannot stay zoomed in or zoomed out. As individuals, we all have a comfort zone – from dwelling deep in details to macro-level engagement. Strategic Leadership requires stretching beyond comfort, developing competence in movement across the understanding continuum – zoomed in and out.

Professor Wind, et al, suggest that the order of process (big picture first, then details, or vice-versa) is not as important as the ability to move back and forth between these two perspectives. They say, "You generally start with a particular vantage point, so the first question to ask is: Where am I standing in relationship to this challenge? If you are at a detached distance, then you may need to zoom in to examine important details. If you are right up against the details of the problem, drowning in its complexity, you need to pull back and look at the broader context. Once you know where you are, you can adjust your perspective to avoid it becoming too fixed."

Drawing upon the lesson from Grandma Olga, seeing our world in the context of a larger universe provides context for Strategic Leadership.

Transcend the center and circumference of the organization

Leading by Cause, Unceasing Re-definition of Normal, Adaptive Disruption, Process Mindset, Seeing Your Organization as Others Do, Winning Hearts and Minds, and Sustainability guide leaders in earning and sustaining relevance. Together, these elements define and transcend the organization; they bring alignment between vision, priorities, and activities. Misalignment leads to unclear business definition, suboptimal performance, and a deleterious impact on relevance. Peter Drucker meant this when he described "the continuous process of making present entrepreneurial (risk-taking) decisions systematically and with the greatest knowledge of their futurity; organizing systematically the efforts needed to carry out these decisions; and measuring the results of these decisions against the expectations through organized, systematic feedback."

This set of contrasts help define context for making present decisions with knowledge of their futurity - Strategic Leadership:

Eliminating Pain Points vs. Execution Progress

I met with the CEO of a regional nonprofit firm to organize a strategic planning meeting with his leadership team. I asked what success looked like for the planning meeting, and he held up his list of the top 10 pain points his company wants to resolve. For him, success was fixing things causing pain for his team.

Removing pain points is a common but misplaced focus. There is nothing wrong with fixing things, but removing pain only gets the business to pain-free, not success.

Strategic Leadership success means performing activities aligned with the company's vision - moving *toward* something intentionally defined, not away from what doesn't work.

The clearer a company is about what it is moving toward, the more successful it will be in executing its strategy. No successful company has a vision of being free from pain points. Strategic Leadership success is greater than the absence of issues.

Making it Work vs. Finding Alignment

When a business is clear in its future state vision, leaders know which activities, decisions, hiring choices or partnerships align, and which are out-of-scope.

Clarity avoids wasting time on activities which will never be a good fit for the business. This applies to the routine, daily activities to which a business applies its resources as well as big picture endeavors – new markets to enter, joint ventures, mergers, or acquisitions.

Struggle vs. Strength

An effective business plan over-weights attention to core competencies – the things your company does best – and steers clear of anything outside that nucleus. This means leaders must be honest with themselves and their organization about what the company does well and what would be better left to others.

Vision, priorities, and activities supporting a strategy, built from strengths, avoid self-imposed distractions. In *Leverage Your Best, Ditch the Rest: The coaching Secrets Top Executives Depend On*, authors Scott Blanchard and Madeleine Homan focus on eliminating "stupid stuff that distracts you and gets in your way."

Their premise: Take full advantage of your strengths while discarding distractions – strategies, activities, events - that get in your way as a leader. This applies to leaders and organizations overall.

A terrific example of playing to strengths is In-N-Out Burger. Their menu exemplifies their strengths – burgers, fries, and shakes. Nothing else. And that focus pays off quite well.

Evidence of In-N-Out Burger playing to their strengths is easy to observe. Count the number of cars waiting in line at an In-N-Out Burger drive-through, then compare that number to observations at any other drive-through restaurant (exception – Chick-fil-A, another competency-focused exemplar). At a recent In-N-Out store grand opening in Aurora, Colorado, people waited in line for up to fourteen hours for burgers, fries, and shakes! Why? In-N-Out plays to their strengths.

Independent vs. Aligned Objectives

Clearly defined employee performance objectives form the basis of Management by Objectives and drive strong organizational performance. Employees with their managers jointly develop performance objectives, creating feelings of co-ownership of activities and results. This strategic management model is effective yet falls short when individual objectives are not aligned with other employees or the organization's priorities.

I managed a marketing team in the government services division of a national bank. My team's responsibilities included developing proposals for financial services – cash management, investments, short-term credit – to local, state, and federal government entities.

Requests for Proposal (RFPs) submitted by government agencies included detailed questions for potential service providers to answer as part of their proposal. We studied the RFP, deconstructed requirements, priced our services based on anticipated activity volume, developed a proposal, then delivered it to the prospective client.

I am convinced I was offered the job assignment because no one else would take it. Prior to me, there were three managers over 18 months. It was a difficult position due to complexities of proposal development and short timeframes to develop and deliver detailed offerings for high-value service contracts.

I quickly learned that proposal delivery deadlines created all-hands-on-deck dramas. Large proposals were 100 pages of service descriptions, legal documents, and pricing information. Input sources came from specialists in product management, pricing, relationship management, risk management, marketing, compliance, and the bank's legal department.

When deadline crunch time approached, there was always some missing ingredient – pricing, product, risk management input - to complete the proposal. Frustration among team members led to finger pointing and ascribing blame for a fire drill. Ironically, every contributor to these proposals claimed to meet their service-level agreement for completing their portion of the work in a timely manner.

How could every department achieve their turn-around time objectives, but the team overall ran out of time meeting proposal submission deadlines? Independent objectives were not synchronized with overall business objectives.

We held an all-team meeting to map-out each step in the proposal development process on a whiteboard. We identified which team member held accountability for each process step, and what their individual objectives (service level agreements for turnaround time) were.

We learned a remarkable lesson. Each team member consistently met their individual turnaround time objectives for sales proposals. Viewed end-to-end, there were gaps between objectives, making it impossible to meet proposal delivery requirements.

Our simple solution – work backward through the proposal development process to determine when each source of input was required. With that information, individual objectives could be defined.

Aligning individual performance objectives with business requirements changed the dynamics of team performance and meeting proposal delivery requirements. The lesson: individual success is not meaningful in a team environment unless activity performance is synchronized.

Dilemma vs. Opportunity

Addressing the question of opportunities in challenging times, eighteenth century German businessman and financier Nathan Rothschild reportedly said: great fortunes are made when cannonballs are falling in the harbor, not just when violins are playing in the ballroom.

Business cycles expand, peak, dip, bottom out, then begin again. There are exceptions, but according to the National Bureau of Economic Research, over 33 business cycles between 1854 and 2009, the average lasted 56 months. These cycles are normal. Defining any point in a cycle good or bad for business misses the Strategic Leadership message. All conditions surface opportunities and challenges. Understanding current conditions in context of the long view helps leaders navigate conditions while capitalizing on expected and unanticipated opportunities.

Next vs. Now

How do leaders focus activities to keep the organization moving forward while lacking clarity from indicators often used as guideposts? Thinking tomorrow, acting today.

Think Tomorrow - Assure your organization's future state vision still fits as you navigate business cycles. If the way your company needs to show-up in the world has changed, it's time to refresh or redefine the vision.

Jeff Bezos, Amazon founder and CEO, believes leaders should think and work in the future. In an article published by *Fast Company*, Bezos discussed decision making and thinking toward the future. He wrote: "None of the people who report to me should really be focused on the current quarter. Right now, I'm working on a quarter that's going to reveal itself sometime [in three years]. You need to be thinking two or three years in advance, and if you are, then why make a hundred decisions today? If I make three good decisions a day, that's enough, and they should just be as high quality as I can make them."[27]

Act Today – Absent a perfect line-of-sight into the future, a clear organizational vision enables leaders and team members to review and refine specific activities supporting business strategies. Strategies that no longer fit the vision or require reconstitution of underlying activities must be redesigned now.

Connecting tomorrow's vision with choices about today's actions requires frequent assessment of results and deconstructing outcomes into their root-cause activities. Cause-based performance analysis (described in Chapter 2, Leading by Cause) requires understanding composition of activities that created results, then assessing performance effectiveness of chosen activities. By understanding the appropriateness of activities engaged in and the effectiveness of strategy execution, leaders can quickly adjust to change outcomes.

London Business School strategy professor, Freek Vermeulen, wrote in the *Harvard Business Review*,[28] "One major reason for the lack of action is that 'new strategies' are often not strategies at all. A real strategy involves a clear set of choices that define what the firm is going to do and what it's *not* going to do. Many strategies fail to get implemented, despite the ample efforts of hard-working people, because they do not represent a set of clear choices."

---

[27] Jeff Bezos: Here's how I make Amazon's highest-stakes decisions, Fast Company, November 23, 2020

[28] Harvard Business Review, Many Strategies Fail Because They're Not Actually Strategies, by Freek Vermeulen, November 08, 2017 - https://hbr.org/2017/11/many-strategies-fail-because-theyre-not-actually-strategies#:~:text=Many%20strategy%20execution%20processes%20fail%20because%20the,not%20have%20something%20worth%20executing.&text=One%20major%20reason%20for%20the,it's%20not%20going%20to%20do.

Strategy matters when the right combination of activities is selected to fulfill an organization's vision, clearly defined, designed, communicated, and deployed through all team members. Balancing today's activities with long-term objectives is essential to making decisions systematically and with the greatest knowledge of their futurity.

Strategic Leadership recognizes that ongoing monitoring of the environment, adaptation as conditions accelerate or slow, consistent, disciplined actions, ongoing comparison of results vs. expectations are ingredients for long-term relevance and success. There is no perfect or permanent strategy. Like GPS rerouting a driver as traffic conditions change, strategy evolves in the path to vision fulfilment.

Closing Thoughts

In *Leading from Where you Are: 7 Themes to Make a Meaningful Impact in Your Work,* I dedicated a chapter to the topic of Making Strategy Matter. The premise: Strategy creates a framework to make decisions and perform activities aimed at a specific target state. Leaders share *connection recognition* responsibility for understanding why their organization does the things it does, from a deductive point of view (big picture down to the details) and inductively (from details up to the big picture). When a leader makes strategy an ongoing dialog rather than an annual or occasional event, they play an active role in bringing the company's vision to life by aligning actions with where the organization wants to go.

Leading from Zero expands the idea to explore how strategy is managed to earn and sustain relevance with stakeholders.

Strategy is the path from current to future state; from today's reality to aspirations which define the organization's vision. While strategy is clearly designed to fulfil the vision, rerouting along the path becomes necessary when conditions change.

My hope is that practicing the Seven Essential Elements of *Leading from Zero* enriches your strategic leadership journey and deepens your toolkit for earning and sustaining relevance with stakeholders.